LEADING WITH
Character, Purpose,
& Passion!

A MODEL FOR SUCCESSFUL
LEADERSHIP AT WORK AND HOME

Roger M. Weis, Ed.D.
Susan M. Muller, Ph.D.

Second Edition

Kendall Hunt
publishing company

Kendall Hunt
publishing company

www.kendallhunt.com
Send all inquiries to:
4050 Westmark Drive
Dubuque, IA 52004-1840

Copyright © 2009, 2014 by Kendall Hunt Publishing Company

ISBN 978-1-4652-4157-3

Printed in the United States of America
10 9 8 7 6 5 4 3 2 1

I dedicate this book to June who lives a life of character, purpose, and passion. Thanks for sharing your heart with me.

Roger M. Weis

CONTENTS

ACKNOWLEDGMENTS

The authors would like to acknowledge and thank a number of people for their guidance on the journey to understanding, teaching, and writing about leadership. They would include Dr. Christopher R. Edginton for his encouragement in the development of our first textbook which included a chapter on leadership. It would also include Dr. Fenwick English, a great teacher and authority on leadership himself who shared his thoughts and beliefs with many, and Dr. Gary Brockway who leads every day with character, purpose, and passion. We also thank the W.K. Kellogg Foundation for their support of our earlier research and publications, along with Jerome and Jeanette Cohen for their kindness and generosity toward earlier works.

A special thank you goes to our research coordinator Dr. Steve Cox for his efforts in locating excellent resources, to research assistant Robin Esau for her expertise and dedication to this work, and to Cooper Levering for his assistance with graphic arts.

We also express our appreciation to those closest to us, our family members Clint Weis, Annika Weis, Riley Weis, Ryder Weis, as well as Edward Green, Karen Lewis, and Katie Ehrisman for their never ending support and encouragement.

A percentage of the profits from each book will go toward supporting charitable organizations.

INTRODUCTION

● ● ● ● ● ●

Each year, a number of books are written around leadership concepts and a number of them are written with great insight and quality. The insight we offer is one developed from years and years of researching, teaching, and practicing leadership concepts then pulling that experience into a focused vision that, if effectively understood, could make an unparalleled difference in your life at home and at work.

We are not offering a magical pill or even a step-by-step process. What we are offering is the opportunity for you to first understand leadership; the opportunity to understand the importance of concepts such as character, purpose, and passion within the realm of leadership; and then understand how to use this realization in making a positive difference with individuals at home and at work!

Many authors and experts within the leadership field concentrate on developing a step-by-step process on becoming a strong leader and while this does have its advantages, it is important to first realize that *character* is the backbone of who a person is. An individual with good *character* is naturally respected, trusted, and followed. When this same person has a clearly defined sense of *purpose* and demonstrates a genuine *passion* for that purpose it can result in an individual who makes a demonstrable difference in the people they come in contact with every day.

While character, purpose, and passion are vital in leadership, it is also important for an individual to have *competencies* in various skill areas or know how to collaborate with individuals with similar or different competencies to make a difference in the lives of others.

An individual who integrates character, purpose, and passion into their leadership style and who has developed competency areas is an individual who will often be trusted and sought after. In the revised *Integrated Leadership and Character Model* the leadership attributes of character, purpose, and passion are incorporated with three different yet interrelated competency areas to produce exciting and long-lasting results when understood and used appropriately. The model will be explained and discussed in detail throughout Part II of this book (see Figure 2, p 33). In the original model (Figure 1), purpose and passion were considered to be part of character (Weis and Gantt 2009).

FIGURE 1   Integrated Leadership and Character (Original Model)

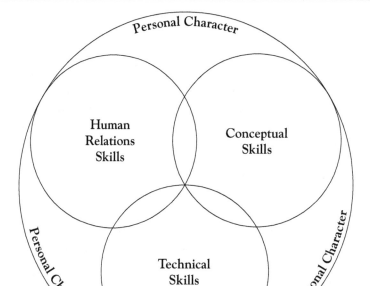

Personal Character	includes traits and values which make each individual unique
Conceptual Skills	identify the critical thinking side of a person and include: vision, decision making and problem solving
Technical Skills	identify a person's specific expertise and include: planning, empowerment, budgeting and stewardship and personal balance
Human Relations Skills	identify a person's ability to interact effectively with others and include: motivation, conflict management, teamwork and valuing diversity
Roger M. Weis and Vernon W. Gantt	

Part I of the book explains the essence of leadership and how important leadership is in the success of groups at home and at work. It lists the four (4) ways individuals can develop as leaders: 1) studying leadership theories, 2) critiquing the lives of leaders, 3) being mentored by a leader, and 4) learning leadership through experiential activities, with specific examples of all four areas before introducing the revised Integrated Leadership and Character Model. Part II of the book describes the revised model in more detail including the importance of character, purpose, and passion and the significance of the interrelated competency areas: conceptual skills, technical skills, and human relation skills in the overall success of a leader at home and at work.

PART I

Combining Character, Purpose, and Passion with Leadership

Because it is vital to the survival of families, communities, businesses, organizations, and even nations, thousands upon thousands of books and articles have been written on the subject of leadership. But what really is leadership anyway and how important is it at home and at work?

The Essence of Leadership

There are as many definitions of leadership as there are authors and experts who describe it. We have a simple, operational definition of leadership that incorporates important aspects of other definitions and works well with forthcoming discussions: *Leadership is about inspiring, guiding, and influencing others to reach goals and make a difference* (Weis and Gantt 2009). It is about recognizing there is a need in a family, community, or organization and accepting the risks (and there are almost always risks) involved in leading others from point A to point B in order to reach hopeful outcomes.

Strong leaders are *inspiring.* They recognize needs and issues that must be addressed and they are excited and committed to resolving or managing those challenges. They not only share that recognition with others but they encourage others to offer their ideas and suggestions on needs and issues and how they might be managed. This is a concept referred to as *shared vision.* Group members in a family or an organization are more likely to buy into the process of addressing various needs if they have offered input into the way issues should be addressed and feel that their input is well received. When group members share the vision and understand the process of reaching that vision an unparalleled synergy develops toward addressing issues and reaching goals.

> ## If your actions inspire others to dream more, learn more, do more and become more, you are a leader.
>
> — *John Quincy Adams*

Successful leaders offer competent *guidance* by developing a shared vision and organizing a process to reach goals effectively and harmoniously. They realize the importance of each individual in reaching group goals and they work hard to *empower* others by providing ideas, training, support, and encouragement which results in a base of *empowerment*. Individuals who are empowered can operate with confidence and competence and feel encouraged to rely more and more on their own initiative. When individuals are encouraged to work with a level of autonomy and freedom, they acquire a higher degree of self-efficacy and believe their efforts are truly making a difference in the organization (Bennis and Townsend 1995).

Finally, and perhaps most importantly, good leaders understand how important it is to use their *influence* to motivate and encourage group members to perform at the highest levels. In fact, many authors equate leadership with influence, which is the ability to affect the attitude and behavior of others through the relationship. Leadership is often defined as the ability to develop followers who will work with a leader to reach goals (Maxwell 1993). One of the most important pieces in that developmental process is having influence so that others will commit to the group's goals and to the processes involved in reaching those goals.

The key to successful leadership today is influence, not authority.

— Kenneth Blanchard

Since influence is so valuable in leadership, it is important to discuss various ways that individuals develop influence with others. One significant way in which we develop influence with others is through the use of *power*. People sometimes think of power as a negative thing, but when it is equated with influence it is perceived as one of the most desirable traits that a leader can have. In a seminal study, French and Raven (1959) identified six sources that power can emanate from: referent power, legitimate power, expert power, reward power, coercive power, and information or persuasive power. These two researchers stated that these sources of power could be used individually or in combination. Let us look at the significance of each source of power in the context of influence.

Individuals often become leaders because they are perceived as having energy and charisma (*referent power*). Leaders with referent power have influence primarily through their personality and likeability and often develop a strong and loyal following from group members.

Others develop a foundation of power primarily through the position or office that they hold (*legitimate power*). People who influence others through an official position can be very persuasive and the authority that goes along with an office can be significant, particularly in hierarchical organizations.

A strong source of influence includes individuals with specific knowledge and skills in particular areas (*expert power*). These individuals are often highly sought after and their leadership level is primarily based on the successes they have experienced.

Individuals who offer rewards for desirable behavior can be very influential (*reward power*). Rewards can be both tangible and intangible in nature and can include salaries, bonuses, and promotions as well as other appropriate forms of appreciation.

Leaders can also use the threat of punishment to move things along effectively (*coercive power*). This power is particularly important in areas of accomplishing goals and in policies that have to do with safety and health issues in families and in organizations. This power should not be under- or overused but must be used skillfully to avoid distrust, hostility, and turmoil.

In making decisions on activities, services, or products, families and other organizations are often faced with difficult decisions and a leader with accurate and updated information can more easily guide the group toward effective decisions (*information* or *persuasive power*).

REFLECTION AND APPLICATION

Since influence and power are so important we're going to ask you to take a few minutes to complete some activities.

First, consider a supervisor you have had in the recent past then list their sources of power in order of priority. How successful was this person with this profile?

_____

_____

_____

_____

Now associate each power with a former United States president.

1. Referent _____

2. Expert _____

3. Legitimate_____

4. Reward_____

5. Coercive _____

6. Persuasive_____

How effective was each president in using a particular source of power?

1. _____

2. _____

3. _____

4. _____

5. _____

6. _____

Next, list your own sources of power in order of priority and consider how successful you are when using each source.

1. _____

2. _____

3. _____

4. _____

5. _____

6. _____

Finally, rent or purchase the movie "Dave" and watch the scenes from when Dave meets the little boy in the homeless shelter to the scene where Dave's security guard interrupts his wife in a meeting (approximately fourteen minutes). Can you identify how each of the six sources of power was used during this period in the movie?

1. Referent _____

2. Expert _____

3. Legitimate_____

4. Reward_____

5. Coercive_____

6. Persuasive_____

This exercise is great to share with colleagues or family members. Spend time discussing any differences in your perceptions of power and its use.

There has been a long-standing discussion on the differences between leaders and managers. *Managers* are usually considered to be individuals with an official position who direct, control, and organize tasks and individuals, whereas *leaders* are individuals who recognize needs and who are willing to take risks in inspiring, guiding, and influencing others to address needs and issues in order to make a difference. Leaders do not necessarily need an official position to be effective. Leaders and managers are important for different reasons. Both *delegate* to others by providing individuals with opportunities to share in responsibilities and authority. Responsibility and authority must be shared in a family or any organization in order for the group to succeed. Good leaders and managers monitor the progress of group members and make adjustments when necessary, a process often called *responsible delegation*. A number of experts believe that families and other organizations should try to develop *leader-managers* (Hitt 1988). These are individuals who know how to organize and direct and also have the ability to inspire individuals to high levels of accomplishment primarily through relationships.

It is our fervent belief that good leaders are made not born. If knowledge and skills can be developed, individuals can acquire the characteristics and skills that are necessary in inspiring, guiding, and influencing others to address needs and meet goals. Many people just want to succeed without necessarily leading the way, so why should anyone want to become a good leader in a family or an organization? If we want to have an influence with our family, with people at work, and with our friends and other community members, we need to become the best leaders we can, for their well-being and for ours.

Begin where you are and do what you can.

— Arthur Ashe

Leadership Development from Within

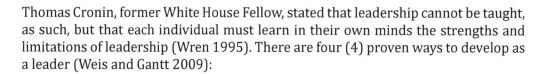

Thomas Cronin, former White House Fellow, stated that leadership cannot be taught, as such, but that each individual must learn in their own minds the strengths and limitations of leadership (Wren 1995). There are four (4) proven ways to develop as a leader (Weis and Gantt 2009):

- Study leadership theories and models, as you are doing now
- Assess the actual lives of leaders for understanding/inspiration
- Ask to be mentored by leaders in your field of interest
- Learn to be a leader through experiential activities and practice

Each of these areas has significance in the overall development of leaders in families and organizations, so let us take a brief look at each.

**To be a great person, walk hand-in-hand
and side-by-side with great people.**

— *Nido Qubein*

Leadership Theories and Models

One way to become a better leader is through the study of leadership theories and models and there are many to consider. We have selected five (5) models that include character as an essential ingredient and that correlate in some respects with the revised *Integrated Leadership and Character Model* (Figure 2, p 33) that will be presented later in this section of the book. These models have been selected for their value to you as a developing leader. Each is reviewed in brief.

Transformational Leadership.   In 1978, Burns suggested that it was possible for individuals to motivate each other toward higher levels of satisfaction and stated that *Transformational Leadership* occurs when one or more persons engage with others in such a way that leaders and followers raise one another to higher levels of motivation and morality (20).

Transformational leadership is a process that is based on fairness and trust; a leader assumes that individuals need commitment and self-fulfillment, empowers individuals, and inspires them to work together to achieve greater and grander goals. Burns (1978) said that "transformational leadership was elevating, and can take place in many aspects of our personal and professional lives" (455). Authors Peters and Waterman (1982) supported Burns and stated that transformational leadership was a great way to inspire individuals, families, and organizations in the pursuit of excellence. The same authors noted that individuals will commit a great deal of themselves to efforts they perceive as worthwhile. Transformational leaders often get involved with group members working closely with others—side by side when possible—in the shared desire to make a difference in a family, institution, or community (Weis and Gantt 2009).

Great leaders have a high regard for achievement, and an even higher regard for people!

— Roger M. Weis

Principle Theory.   The idea of leaders incorporating virtues, values, or principles in their leadership style has been thought about, written about, and practiced for centuries and is now generally referred to as the *Principle Theory.* Plato and Aristotle noted that leaders should place less emphasis on rules and more on the importance of developing good habits and considered virtues such as justice, prudence, courage, and temperance. Later, Christian writers added virtues to the list such as treating others equally and making virtue a quality with both earthly and heavenly rewards attached. Virtues are considered qualities that, when followed, allow us to reach worthy goals and to refrain from temptations and distractions (MacIntyre 1981).

More recently, virtues have been considered by many to be values, or the principles that guide our lives. Character traits such as honesty and patience have often been mentioned as critical parts of effective leadership. In the 1980s and 1990s, Stephen Covey (1989) expanded the idea that effective living and leadership could only be achieved if individuals integrated principles such as *integrity, honesty, service,* and *excellence* into their daily activities. He stated that people could maintain these principles by developing certain habits, or purposeful systems of maintaining principles in all that they do. Leading with principles can result in strong, trusting relationships. Stephen Covey's book, *The 7 Habits of Highly Effective People* (1989) is a wonderful resource for leading with principles and is highly recommended.

Collaborative Leadership.   A more contemporary style of leadership, *Collaborative Leadership,* involves bringing people together to build trust, cooperation, and communication. The concept emphasizes sharing ideas and listening, understanding, and often acting on the input of those involved. Eisler (1995) stated that collaborative leaders avoid dominating and directing approaches and develop a nurturing environment of support and trust. Group members are treated as important and worthwhile individuals.

In the book *The Flight of the Buffalo,* Belasco and Stayer (1993) discuss how collaborative leadership also has to do with taking turns leading, depending on circumstances and different situations. They describe good leaders as those who empower others to lead under specific conditions and who do not feel threatened by others taking a leadership position. The same authors make an interesting comparison of collaborative leadership and geese; geese communicate continually during flight and take turns leading when one becomes tired or the situation changes in some other way. In *collaborative leadership*, effective communication and trust are encouraged as is the sharing of leadership. Individuals are encouraged to accept positions of leadership when it is appropriate and helpful for the goals of the group.

Invitational Leadership.   In the book *Becoming an Invitational Leader: A New Approach to Professionalism and Personal Success,* Purkey and Siegel (2003) develop a holistic and dynamic model of leadership suggesting that leaders need to invite their colleagues, family members, and others to participate in happier, more effective relationships. They suggest that leaders should practice four specific values or guiding principles in inviting others to participate in more successful processes and activities; these are *respect, trust, optimism,* and *intentionality.*

One of the most important aspects of leadership is letting others know that we value them and one of the most important ways that we do that is by acting *respectful* of others by being courteous, expressing appreciation, and care. The importance of respect should come into play on a day-to-day basis and is certainly important during times of crisis. By *trusting* others we are letting them know that we trust their abilities and integrity. Trust is created when families and organizations share a set of values and although there is a certain level of vulnerability attached to trust, there is a greater strength in trusting relationships. *Optimists* tend to expect the very best from the human spirit and often work diligently to turn negatives into positives. Optimists believe that each individual, family, and organization can and should be striving toward their full potential.

Intentionality is a key part of this leadership concept because invitational leaders intentionally focus on being respectful, trustworthy, and optimistic. This focus encourages individuals, families, and organizations to be their very best and to grow stronger together.

Servant Leadership. Robert K. Greenleaf is credited with a theory of leadership in which an individual begins with the natural feeling of wanting to serve others first. That individual recognizes the desire to serve and continues on to make a conscious decision to develop as a leader. Greenleaf designates this theory as *servant leadership*, a concept he developed after reading Hermann Hesse's *Journey to the East* (Greenleaf 1970). In this book, a group of men are on a mythical journey and are sustained by their servant Leo who provides various tasks for the group while maintaining their spirits with his optimism and joyful nature. All goes well on the journey until Leo disappears and the group and their journey fall into disarray for a time. Years later, it is learned that Leo was actually a noble leader who sponsored the journey in the first place.

According to Greenleaf, a *servant-leader's* passion is to make sure that people's needs are being served and while doing so they are growing stronger and more competent and confident as the *servant-leader* works to empower them. A *servant-leader* works for his or her people and does everything possible to help them accomplish goals and be successful. A good *servant-leader* places the well-being of others above oneself and often directs credit for successes to others.

It is high time the ideal of success be replaced by the ideal of service.

— Albert Einstein

REFLECTION AND APPLICATION

There are many, many other important models and theories regarding leadership.

Discuss with your co-workers who in your organization practices each one of these theories. How do they act? What do they do to make you identify them with the theory which you think best matches their leadership style?

1. Transformational _____

2. Principle _____

3. Collaborative _____

4. Invitational _____

5. Servant_____

Ask family members about people, past or present, who live up to the leadership style descriptions provided in these pages. Why were or are those people considered examples of the theory?

1. Transformational _____

2. Principle _____

3. Collaborative _____

4. Invitational _____

5. Servant_____

Once you learn the stories of current or past leaders, share them with new members of your work team.

Are there other leadership models you are familiar with and fond of?

_____

_____

_____

_____

What do you like about the model(s)?

_____

_____

_____

_____

_____

_____

Is character an important aspect of the model(s)? If not, could/should character be integrated in the model(s)?

_____

_____

_____

_____

_____

_____

Each of the models above is an excellent example of the importance of principles and character in the leadership process involving families and organizations. We will come back to some of these models later in this book.

There are many other important models and theories regarding leadership. Discuss with family members who in your family resembles the descriptions included in one or more of these theories. How do they act? What actions made you think of them when you read about this theory? At work, ask about people they know who live up to the descriptions provided in these pages. How might those people be considered examples of the theory? Once you learn the stories of current or past leaders, share them with new members of your work team. Are there other leadership models you are familiar with and fond of? Is character an important aspect of the model(s)? If not, could/should character be integrated into the model(s)?

Assessing the Lives of Leaders Past

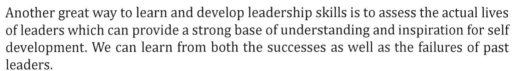

Another great way to learn and develop leadership skills is to assess the actual lives of leaders which can provide a strong base of understanding and inspiration for self development. We can learn from both the successes as well as the failures of past leaders.

According to *Lao Tzu*, a Chinese philosopher who lived in sixth century BC, leaders should place the well-being of others above themselves and should serve more as a facilitator rather than a task maker (Wren 1995). He believed that leaders should be nurturing, caring, and interested in the individuals being led and that credit for success should be directed toward others. *Lao Tzu* also believed that when circumstances required a leader to take a stronger stance, group members should still feel as if they were being assisted rather than led, so they could maintain a sense of autonomy. It is easy to see that Lao Tzu was an *empowering* individual and that his type of leadership led to mutual trust, motivation, and empowerment for those involved.

Thomas Jefferson was born into a prominent Virginia family in 1743; his father was a wealthy plantation owner; and his mother was from distinguished Scottish and English families (Koch and Peden 1993). He was the author of the *Declaration of Independence*, the founder of the University of Virginia, and the third President of this country. He was brilliant as a statesman, scientist, inventor, educator, and architect. His vast knowledge and statesmanlike abilities assisted him greatly in moving the country forward, toward the birth of independence from England (Meacham 2012). His southern, aristocratic culture however led to a contradiction for the man who wrote, "We hold these truths to be self-evident, that all men are created equal, that they are endowed by their Creator with certain unalienable Rights, that among these are Life, Liberty, and the pursuit of Happiness" in the *Declaration of Independence*. For even as he wrote these words, he continued to buy and sell slaves; and continued to do so even later when serving as President. Jefferson will always be remembered as one of the greatest leaders of the country but he will also be remembered as a man of significant contradictions.

In the early 1800s, *Harriett Tubman* grew up as a slave on the eastern shore of Maryland and learned at a very young age how it felt to be oppressed and devalued (Clinton 2004). She had to work in the fields of the plantation as a young girl where she lived from early in the morning to dusk and was even hired out to other families for cleaning, weaving, and caring for children (Petry 1955). As she became a young woman, Tubman grew determined not to live life as a slave and made the decision to escape to the North although her husband John refused to accompany her. Her escape was assisted by the Underground Railroad, which was little more than a loosely organized group of people who helped with shelter and food for travels ahead. Even though Tubman had made it safely to the North, she kept returning to the South again and again to lead other slaves to freedom despite the considerable dangers involved. Tubman became the first black individual to conduct on the Underground Railroad; previous escapes had always been led by white men (Clinton 2004). Harriett Tubman led with compassion, conviction, and determination.

Each sunset calls your heart to seek light, warmth and freedom for all who are enslaved.

— Roger M. Weis

Clara Barton was born on Christmas day in 1821 and grew up in Oxford, Massachusetts, and was rather shy as a youngster (Boylson 1955). As a young adult, she became a teacher and was admired by her students for her caring ways and determination to be involved with their lives even out of the classroom. When war broke out between the states, Barton worked as a nurse saving countless lives and often working from daybreak to dusk. Later on, while visiting in Europe, she learned about the International Red Cross (IRC), an organization that provided relief efforts for individuals during times of upheaval. When she returned, she began organizing the American version of the IRC to provide relief services for victims of disaster. She was soon appointed to be president of the National Red Cross, which later became the American Red Cross (*The Biography Channel Website* 2013). Her caring nature, vision, and determination would change the shape of a nation and the lives of millions of people for decades to come.

George A. Custer was a graduate of West Point and first served as a general in the Civil War; and was considered by many as a hero for leading troops against the Confederate cavalry and defending the Union Army from attack from Confederate infantrymen (Utley 1988). His superiors described him as a warrior who fought with courage, conviction, and an unparalleled fury and focus on victory. As a matter of fact, had it not been for a place in Montana called Little Big Horn, he could well have become President Custer because of his competencies and determination. After the Civil War, Custer was sent by his government to protect pioneering Americans as they moved West. He became famous for his successes fighting the Indians, but Little Big Horn came to be his undoing when Custer and all of the men in his unit were lost (Philbrick 2010). Overconfident from past successes, Custer underestimated the strength of his enemy and overestimated his own competencies and the will of his troops, resulting in his demise.

As a youngster in Tuscumbia, Alabama, in the early 1900s, *Helen Keller* lived a fairly normal childhood until she reached the age of nineteen months, when a fever she developed left her both deaf and blind (Richards 1968). With limited capabilities for healthy communication, she became something of a behavior problem until she was introduced to Anne Sullivan.

Sullivan herself had almost become blind and overcame many obstacles to become a teacher of the blind, the deaf, and the mute. Because of Sullivan's skills and determination with Keller, Helen began to read and write by using Braille and grew calmer as her communication opportunities increased. Eventually, Keller mastered four different types of alphabets and wrote her own story about growing up with so many challenges and the story became a book, *The Story of My Life,* which was printed in fifty different languages. Keller went on to encourage thousands of others with similar afflictions and was deeply involved with the American Foundation for the Blind. She also wrote *Teacher* as a tribute to her teacher and mentor, Anne Sullivan. By using compassion, love, and skill, Anne Sullivan and Helen Keller worked together to overcome extraordinary circumstances that changed the lives of thousands of others.

Ask migrant farm workers who their hero is and they will often answer emphatically with the name *Cesar Chavez* (Levy 1975). Chavez grew up in the town of Gila Bend, Arizona, where his family owned land and businesses. But the Depression of 1929 left them virtually penniless and they had to leave their home and begin a life of picking crops. The conditions in the labor camps where the Chavez family was forced to live were often horrible with no electricity, heat, or running water. The school system the Chavez children attended was considered racist and children were actually punished for speaking Spanish.

Later in life and following a stint in the U.S. Navy, Chavez took a position with the Community Service Organization where he registered people to vote and learned about power, organizing agencies, and initiating sit-ins. He carried these attributes with him when he organized the National Farm Workers Association to successfully work for decent wages and benefits for ordinary farm workers. In spite of working in opposition to the powerful California Growers Association, the Teamsters Union, and the AFL-CIO, Chavez maintained nonviolent strategies to win fairness for farm workers. Chavez employed organizational skills, determination, and a commitment to the common good to overcome seemingly insurmountable obstacles.

Dr. Martin Luther King, Jr. was born January 15, 1929, in Atlanta, Georgia, as the son of a minister (Frady 2002). In 1954, he became the minister of the Dexter Avenue Baptist Church in Montgomery, Alabama, at the young age of twenty-five. He graduated from Morehouse College and Crozer Theological Seminary and completed his doctoral studies at Boston University in 1955. Dr. King was inspired by Mahatma Gandhi's success with nonviolent activism and visited Gandhi's birthplace in India.

He returned with the strong sense of nonviolent resistance as a weapon in the fight against oppressed people in their struggle for human dignity (Weis and Gantt 2009).

Dr. King became the most prominent leader in the Civil Rights Movement in the United States. From organizing the 1955 Montgomery Bus Boycott to the 1963 *I Have a Dream* speech during the March on Washington, he was the guiding force for a generation of people from every walk of life in pursuit of civil rights for Americans. He had a very long list of accomplishments in this country and beyond. Martin Luther King, Jr. was recognized with the Nobel Peace Prize in 1964. Martyred by an assassin's bullet on April 4, 1968, he had dedicated his life for the cause of social justice and fairness for all (Montefiore 2005).

It is important to assess other leaders to determine the kinds of character traits and areas of expertise that appeal to us. The leaders described above had high levels of character and various areas of expertise and most often they incorporated their character and expertise for the common good successfully. In some instances, we can also see where a flaw in character or a skill area can lead to failure. When we see character and skills in others that we admire, we can strive to emulate those areas. When we see flaws in their character and skills, we can try to avoid those deficiencies. We can learn from their successes and from their failures.

There are thousands and thousands of leaders we come to respect and admire. Some of them are in the next room, down the street or across town; they are a part of our families and our social circles. Others are written about and discussed locally, nationally, and beyond.

REFLECTION AND APPLICATION

There are thousands and thousands of "leaders" we come to respect and admire. Some of them are in the next room, down the street, or across town; they are a part of our families and our social circles. Others are written about and discussed locally, nationally, and beyond.

Who are some other leaders who are especially important to you?

_____

_____

_____

_____

_____

_____

_____

_____

_____

_____

What do you like about them?

_____

_____

_____

_____

_____

_____

_____

_____

_____

_____

What have you learned from them? Explain each example.

_____

_____

_____

_____

_____

_____

_____

How important was character in your selection of each person?

_____

_____

_____

_____

_____

_____

_____

_____

How can these people help you be a better leader at work, at home?

_____

_____

_____

_____

_____

_____

Mentoring and Leadership

Another way that we can all develop our leadership abilities is through the process of *mentoring.* Individuals can become more successful at home or at work by being supported and helped by others more experienced than they. A mentor can provide direct guidance and support as well as offer suggestions regarding outside resources such as training opportunities, workshops, seminars, and even counseling or coaching. Successful mentoring can only take place in the context of a trusting relationship. Individuals involved in mentoring must enter a genuine communication process characterized by good interaction, a problem-solution mindset, an attempt to develop new ideas, and a collaborative thought process (Bokeno and Gantt 2000).

There are four key components in a good mentoring relationship: *caring, sharing, correcting, and connecting* (Gantt 1997). Mentoring is not an assignment to be initiated, it only works when individuals develop a genuine trust for each other and *care* about the well-being of the other person. That concern for another individual can be demonstrated in part by *sharing* the kind of information or strategies that can be beneficial in a number of different types of situations. Another important component of mentoring is *correcting* another person when they are behaving or thinking in negative, dysfunctional, irrational, or self-defeating ways. This is the trickiest of the four key components because it can sometimes be interpreted as criticism and needs to be implemented carefully and skillfully. Finally, a good mentoring relationship includes *connecting* individuals to others who may be helpful in their growth as a people and as leaders.

Almost all of us have been coached, empowered, and mentored by others. Who comes to mind when you think of someone who has spent a good deal of time offering guidance and support for you? What were some of the most helpful sort of things they did for you? Where would we be without our mentors?

The greatest good you can do for another is not just to share your riches but to reveal to him his own.

— Benjamin Disraeli

REFLECTION AND APPLICATION

Almost all of us have been coached, empowered, and mentored by others.

Who comes to mind when you think of someone who has spent a good deal of time offering you guidance and support?

_____

_____

_____

_____

_____

_____

_____

_____

_____

_____

What were some of the most helpful suggestions they made to you?

_____

_____

_____

_____

_____

_____

_____

_____

_____

_____

_____

_____

What can/should you do to be a better mentor for others?

_____

_____

_____

_____

_____

_____

_____

_____

_____

_____

_____

What benefits have you personally recognized from being mentored at work or at home?

_____

_____

_____

_____

_____

_____

_____

_____

_____

_____

_____

_____

Learning to be a Leader through Experience and Practice

Another way for individuals to develop as leaders is to participate in activities that provide opportunities for skill and character development through *experiential learning* processes. This is considered by many to be one of the best ways to learn about various content areas; incorporating that knowledge through practical experience activities. Businesses, nonprofit organizations, and educational institutions often provide internships or student teaching opportunities for individuals. Students take what they have learned in classrooms, seminars, and workshops and, with the help of experienced supervisors, modify that knowledge to fit the needs of the organization. One of the fastest growing pedagogies in educational institutions and service organizations is *service learning.* Service learning is a field experience that combines community service with various learning objectives (Weis and Long 2011). Studies indicate that individuals make significant strides in areas of personal growth, career development, social development, and cognitive development through service learning activities.

Families should be, and often are, involved with experiential learning activities. A father may provide coaching for his daughter in the knowledge and skills of a sport, for instance, and support further practice and involvement in team sports. A mother might teach her son the importance of character including the importance of respect and service and get involved with him in serving lunch at a local homeless shelter. Whether experiential learning takes place in a home, a business, or another setting, it is very important that instruction of content area is delivered effectively and that the experiences are supported and monitored and assessed appropriately.

Finally, it is important to remember that we need to practice, monitor, and adjust the leadership concepts we have learned time and again until they are most effective for us. And once they are effective, we need to practice, monitor, and adjust repeatedly; leadership development only stops when you let it stop!

**I hear and I forget.
I see and I remember.
I do and I understand.**

— Confucius

REFLECTION AND APPLICATION

Think about some experiential learning situations you have been involved with recently or in the past.

What are some of the lessons you have learned or are learning from those experiences?

_____

_____

_____

_____

_____

_____

_____

_____

_____

_____

_____

_____

_____

_____

_____

_____

_____

_____

_____

_____

_____

_____

_____

Will you be able to use these lessons in being a better leader in the future? How so?

_____

_____

_____

_____

_____

_____

_____

_____

_____

_____

_____

_____

_____

_____

_____

_____

_____

_____

_____

_____

_____

_____

_____

_____

_____

_____

_____

Understanding the Integrated Leadership and Character Model

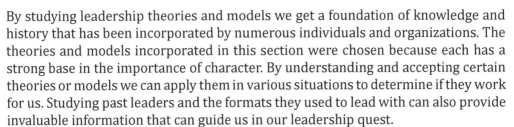

By studying leadership theories and models we get a foundation of knowledge and history that has been incorporated by numerous individuals and organizations. The theories and models incorporated in this section were chosen because each has a strong base in the importance of character. By understanding and accepting certain theories or models we can apply them in various situations to determine if they work for us. Studying past leaders and the formats they used to lead with can also provide invaluable information that can guide us in our leadership quest.

Additionally, a great way to develop as a leader is when one individual takes a genuine interest in the development of another and provides concern, support, and information; in other words, works hard at mentoring and empowering that individual and encouraging them to be the best they can possibly be. This requires a great deal of trust and give and take on the part of both individuals. Finally, it is important to test the theories that have been proposed and the stories and lessons that have been learned in a structured, experiential learning format; where concepts can be applied to various situations and a seasoned supervisor, teacher, mom, dad, or friend can help a developing leader become stronger and more enlightened.

By studying leadership theories and models we establish a foundation of knowledge and history gleaned from the experiences of numerous individuals and organizations. The theories and models presented in this section were selected because each has a strong base in the importance of character. By understanding and accepting certain theories and models we can apply them in various situations and make modifications to fit our specific circumstances that will improve our outcomes. Studying past leaders and the formats they used to lead successfully also provides insight that will guide us in our leadership quest.

Mentoring is another great way to develop leadership skills. When an experienced individual takes a genuine interest in the development of another person, providing concern, support, and information, this empowers that individual and encourages him or her to be the best he/she can possibly be. Successful mentorship requires a great deal of trust and give and take on the part of both individuals. The focus should remain on testing the theories that have been proposed and the stories and lessons that have been learned in a structured, experiential learning format; where concepts can be applied to various situations and a seasoned supervisor, teacher, parent, or friend can help an individual become a stronger and more enlightened leader.

It is important to consciously work at developing leadership skills by studying various theories and models and following these study sessions with the careful application of those models in one's life. The theories and models included in this text were purposefully selected due to the strong connection each makes between leadership and character. *Character* is the foundation of a person and is a central element in how one person might influence another. Leadership models too often ignore the importance of character in the overall scheme of leading and influencing others.

Personal character includes the traits and values that distinguish one person from another; it involves being true to the standard or standards a person has set to govern his or her life (Weis and Gantt 2004). Character without *purpose* and *passion*, however, lacks energy and direction; these two attributes must be included in a leadership formula to result in developing a strong and effective leader. Effective leadership also requires one to be knowledgeable and skilled in several competency areas, or to be able to connect with individuals skilled in these areas in order to make a difference in the lives of others.

In Part II, the revised model will be explained in more detail with suggestions and strategies to be used for building successful leadership skills.

PART
II

Leading with Character, Purpose, and Passion at Home and at Work

Why Should Anyone Pursue Leadership Skills?

To effect change or have any influence on family members, organizational constituents, or community members, becoming a leader is a requirement, not an option. Being the best leader possible takes planning, thought, and determination. Becoming a successful leader at home and at work is the overall goal of the Integrated Leadership and Character Model, which provides a structure for self-assessment and development for individuals in both settings. It can also be used for assessing and developing others.

The Revised Integrated Leadership and Character Model (Figure 2) was developed as a framework for including the three leadership attributes including human relations skills, conceptual skills, and technical skills. When the model is understood and applied, it can make an unparalleled difference in how we lead and influence those around us (Weis and Gantt 2009). The model may be used as an assessment and development tool for self-improvement, as well as an assessment and development concept for families and organizations. The model has been used nationally and internationally in the selection and training of staff members in various organizations and has been included in textbooks and journals nationally and internationally. The model was developed through a three-year research project involving hundreds of individuals, community leaders, and educators (Weis and Gantt 2009).

According to the model:

- To be successful, leaders must have the kind of personal character (traits and values), sense of purpose, and level of passion that is important in leading a family or organization successfully.
- Additionally, they must possess or develop appropriate levels of conceptual, technical, and human relations skills (Katz 1995), or be able to collaborate with those who possess them.
- The interaction and effectiveness of the three skill and knowledge areas or competencies are dependent on the character, purpose, and passion of the leader.

In the original model (Figure 1, p. x), purpose and passion were subsumed within or understood to be a part of character, but each of these aspects is extremely important. Therefore, the revised model includes these areas in a deservedly prominent role. Next, we will look at how the model might play out at work or at home.

To develop effective products or services in any organization, a leader must have a sense of what the customer, clients, or members need and want *(conceptual skills)*. This understanding helps to develop the vision, which provides the path to be followed. The leader must be able to follow-up on this vision with competent skills in planning and implementing products or participate in programs or services *(human relation skills)*. When good leaders are not well versed in competency areas, they

FIGURE 2   Integrated Leadership and Character Revised Model

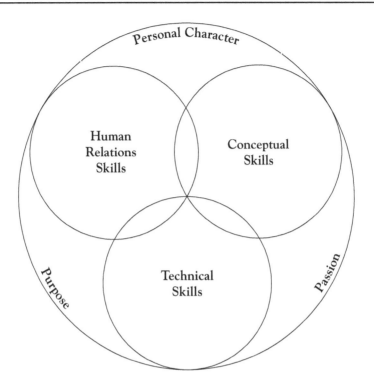

Personal Character	includes traits and values which make each individual unique
Purpose	includes a clear understanding and focus on the mission of a group
Passion	includes a total commitment for the group's purpose
Conceptual Skills	identify the critical thinking side of a person and include: vision, decision making and problem solving
Technical Skills	identify a person's specific expertise and include: planning, empowerment, budgeting and stewardship and personal balance
Human Relations Skills	identify a person's ability to interact effectively with others and include: motivation, conflict management, teamwork and valuing diversity
Roger M. Weis and Vernon W. Gantt	

must be skilled in collaborating with those who are. The more trusted, focused, and determined an individual is to make the product or program work *(character, purpose, and passion)* the more likely it is that the product or program will succeed. The same process should work for any activity in any organization (Weis, Rogers, and Broughton 2004).

The model works in a similar way in a family setting. Family leaders must learn what family members need and want *(conceptual skills)*, and they must be able to communicate and motivate members of their family toward these needs *(human relation skills).* The more respected, focused, and determined the leader *(character, purpose, and passion),* the more likely family members will be to buy into the process for achieving family goals together.

After the foundation of the model is understood, it is essential to amplify the individual components and understand how they link character, purpose, and passion at home and at work. In the rest of Part II, the three main leadership attributes of the model are explained in more detail, emphasizing the interrelationship of the competency areas that are important in making a difference with others, integrating the model in the contexts of home and work. This explanation begins with the leadership attributes.

How Character, Purpose, and Passion Holds the Model Together

Personal character is the essence of who a person is and includes the traits and values that define an individual and distinguishes him or her from others. A leader with good character can be trusted, respected, and counted on to get the job done effectively within the framework of the shared values of all group members. Additionally, leaders must focus on the group's shared vision or *purpose,* and have an absolute *passion* for that aspiration. This enthusiasm for the envisioned outcome will provide the requisite energy to move the group forward. Although the three interrelated skill areas shown in Figure 2 are critical to the success of any group, the interaction and effectiveness of those competency areas are dependent on the character, purpose, and passion of group leaders and of other members of the group.

The Importance of Character, Purpose, and Passion in Leading

Within the context of leadership, personal character, purpose, and passion are each important in their own way. Leaders with good character are respected and often followed. Good leaders help group members maintain a focus on the purpose of the family or organization, and often demonstrate an immeasurable passion for that purpose, which can be contagious for other group members. Although these three attributes are interrelated, just as with the three competency areas, each characteristic will be reviewed separately in the next section.

Personal Character is a Critical Aspect in Leadership

The role that character plays in leadership cannot be overstated. Merriam-Webster defines character as one of the attributes or features that make up and distinguish an individual. *Personal character* includes the traits and values an individual chooses and develops to govern his or her life. These attributes do not select us, we choose the traits and values we deem to be important. An individual with the greatest skills and competencies can fail miserably if there are significant flaws in their character—this has been proven time and again throughout history. Although no one is expected to be perfect, leaders must make life choices that will enable them to lead effectively and enable others along the way.

Personal Character

Human Relations Skills

Conceptual Skills

Technical Skills

Purpose

Passion

According to Dr. Ronald Riggio, the Henry R. Kravis Professor of Leadership and Organizational Psychology at Claremont McKenna College, leaders are more made or developed than born. He points out that despite the inherent predispositions toward leadership possessed by some individuals, effective leaders actually sharpen their skills through real-life experiences and engaging in learning and self-development activities (Riggio 2009).

There are two types of leaders, and there is a need for both. First, the transformational leader is one who lifts people up, inspires, and empowers others to perform well beyond that which they have already achieved. The second type involves the transactional leaders, who are noted for getting things done, through and with others (Tracy and Chee 2013). Regardless of the category of leader that you aspire to become, the leadership model presented here will provide a foundation for the skills and competencies required to succeed.

First we will look at the traits and values we believe are essential for effective character, and then we will discuss ways to develop character.

Traits and Values Critical for Good Character

There are as many lists of important traits and values for character as there are experts and authors. Traits are those characteristics that make us unique and values are the principles that guide our lives. We have developed a blended, select list of traits and values from experts and references that we believe is essential for strong character. These references include the Six Pillars of Character from Character Counts (Character Counts 2007), a list of attributes important for leadership endorsed by 17,000 individuals from 62 countries from the GLOBE Study (House, Hanges, Javidan, Dorfman, and Gupta (Eds.) 2004), a selection of character traits from leadership authors John Maxwell (Maxwell 1999) and Stephen Covey (Covey 1989), suggested attributes on character from the book *The Leadership Challenge* (Kouzes and Posner 2002), and our own list from the textbook *Knowledge & Skill Development in Nonprofit Organizations* (2009). Although not intended to be all-inclusive, we believe these traits and values are absolutely necessary for successful leadership at home and at work:

1. *Commitment.*   Commitment refers to having a sense of purpose and meaning. Being committed requires active engagement in work, to follow through on one's responsibilities (Gorrow and Muller 2008, 14).

    One of the most important attributes that an effective leader must have is a very strong commitment to the mission of the group and to individual group members. As long as the mission of the group is clear and encompassing, then all activities can be designed toward that mission, and it is the leader's responsibility to ensure that group members remain focused on the mission. (The importance of mission or *purpose* will be discussed separately and in detail later in the book.) It is also critical that a leader frequently communicates, verbally and by his or her actions, a commitment to the success and well-being of each and every member of the group. Commitment requires the investing of time and energy toward something you want to pursue and is most successful when backed by inspiration.

    When a leader exhibits a commitment to the mission, as well as to individuals within the organization, this increases cohesion by strengthening the bonds between group members. Leaders demonstrate a genuine interest and concern for their associates by consistently displaying high levels of compassion and empathy, and by use of social skills, which results in higher levels of commitment among their followers. Commitment by a leader is crucial and adds a high level of legitimacy to the purpose of the family or organization.

2. *Integrity.*   One of the strongest characteristics necessary for good leadership is integrity. Honesty and integrity are universally seen as desired traits for those aspiring to leadership roles. Evidence of this is reported by Kouzes and Posner (2007) in the Leadership Challenge. These authors note that on surveys of over 75,000 people around the globe asking what people most look for and admire in a leader. Honesty, which aligns with integrity, was the leadership characteristic most often cited by respondents. This means that group members and others will be able to trust a leader to be honest, responsible, and effective in helping his or her group reach their goals.

   Integrity inspires confidence from others, and it is so much easier for groups to be successful when leadership has a proven track record for being trusted and dependable. Possessing integrity also implies that a leader will be fair and treat each individual with respect. While no one is expected to be perfect, if and when a leader errs, it is crucial to correct that mistake quickly, genuinely, and appropriately and to learn from that experience.

Leadership is a combination of strategy and character. If you must be without one, be without the strategy.

— Gen. H. Norman

---

3. *Concern.*   Leaders who express genuine concern for group members and others associated with a group's mission help them feel cared for and important, and make it much easier for them to work toward the purpose of the group. Expressing empathy, consideration, and a real interest in the lives of others demonstrates that individuals are just as important as the group's mission, and helps members feel a real sense of belonging. These behaviors also help to strengthen the bonds between leaders and group members.

   The authors of *The Truth About Leadership* emphasize the importance of concern and caring in the process of leading when quoting a successful business leader who stated that "All things being equal, we will work harder and more effectively for people we like. And we like them in direct proportion to how they make us feel." (Kouzes and Posner 2010, 137).

4. *Competence.* Competencies in conceptual, technical, and human relations skills are the nuts and bolts of successful group dynamics. Leaders should be aware of these areas and understand how they interact among the members of their group. Competencies can be developed or learned; individual group members can and should work together in improving or enhancing various skills to help achieve the goals. The leader does not need to be an expert in all three areas in the context of the wide variety of situations encountered by the group. Instead, good leaders must know how to blend the skill areas, and how to collaborate with others to bring required expertise into the group when necessary.

5. *Communication.* Effective leaders listen and attempt to understand each group member's communication, taking action when appropriate. In a successful organization everyone knows what it is that they are trying to accomplish. Poor communication leads to a lack of direction. If people become unsure about what they should be doing, they become insecure, engage in politics, and demotivated (Tracy and Chee 2013, 14). Effective leadership requires displaying personal competence at times and seeking information or assistance at others times, and most importantly being able to consistently select the correct course of action.

6. *Determination.* It seems as if each day of our lives includes hurdles and obstacles that we have to overcome. Successful leaders work well with others to develop methods to address issues and to move past situations that impede progress toward the group's goals. Good leaders are not easily swayed in the presence of what may seem like overwhelming odds and work hard, patiently, and diligently at finding just the right solution to potential pitfalls. It is important too that leaders help group members stay together as a team and maintain a confident attitude while addressing problems. Groups that succeed over and over again in the face of adversity are strengthened by the experiences and more and more willing to take on challenges when they know there is a genuine resolve to be successful.

Always make a total effort, even when the odds are against you.

— Arnold Palmer

7. *Flexibility.*   Being flexible, or going with the flow, is one form of adaptation. Consider the "mind like water" concept martial artists teach. Picture a stone tossed into a pool of water. As the stone drops into it, the water reshapes and adapts to the force, dissipating it to return quickly to its original calm. The water does not anticipate or ignore the stone, but responds to it when needed and only as much as necessary. When stones are tossed into your pool, try to emulate the water and adapt as needed (Insel and Roth 2008).

    Because there are so many complexities involved in leading a family or an organization, leaders must be able to effectively coordinate numerous activities at the same time. Good leaders recognize the many different dimensions involved in group dynamics and are able to coordinate the available resources to enable success in many different areas, often at or around the same time. The leader must be able to adapt to change and, in some instances, initiate change (Weis and Gantt 2009). He or she must be able to assume a number of different roles pertaining to different situations, individuals, and relationships. Once a graduate who took a position as a program coordinator for a youth and human service organization compiled a list of twenty-five roles he had taken on in his new position; they included counselor, coach, teacher, nurse, negotiator, custodian, accountant, and policeman among others. Successful groups require a leader who can serve with flexibility.

8. *Courage.*   British Prime Minister Winston Churchill thought that courage was the most esteemed human quality "because it is the quality which guarantees all others." Leadership requires taking risks in order to make improvements or to initiate new activities, services, or products. Courage is inspirational, and group members who sense that their leader is willing to take a chance to make a difference are more likely to become comfortable with taking risks as well. If you were to speak with successful business or sports leaders about failure, they would say that they did a lot of things that didn't work initially or that they struck out a number of times. Despite numerous failures, most eventually succeeded because they had the courage to try something again and again until it worked. Remaining true to a principle in spite of the difficulty helps to promote courage among others in the group.

    According to Kathy Reardon, professor of management and organization at the University of Southern California's Marshall School of Business, courageous action involves taking a calculated risk (2007). Good leaders learn to make bold decisions through a process that takes time to develop. The point is that courage is not an innate quality that great leaders are born with; it is a skill that is learned and honed over time. Refining the decision-making process requires lots of practice, so aspiring leaders must recognize that mistakes will be made and have the courage to persevere despite this inevitability.

> # Life has its own hidden forces which you can only discover by living.
>
> — *Soren Kierkegaard*

9. *Win-Win Approach.* Leaders should try to approach each situation, conflict, or activity with the sense that everyone will benefit from what is about to transpire. In his book *The 7 Habits of Highly Effective People,* Stephen Covey's 4th habit was *Think Win-Win* because he realized that each person involved in a situation would feel much more comfortable with decisions and directions if they were mutually beneficial and therefore be more supportive of action plans designed around those decisions and goals (1989). When there is a win-win culture in any family or organization, members feel a stronger connection to the group and are often more committed to the overall purpose and goals. Leaders must create an environment that rewards actions and outcomes that are mutually beneficial.

    To create win-win situations it is important to first view the situation from each person's perspective. What would a winning scenario look like for each stakeholder? Can a goal or process be devised that helps everyone achieve something of value? Clarify your goals and establish priorities. What might or must be compromised to get everyone working toward a common goal? If you are able to establish common ground, accomplishments will be more significant and will be shared and celebrated by a larger audience.

    The win-win approach is an important concept and will be discussed again in a later section.

10. *Citizenship.* One of the most important values that any group should have is a desire to make their community and the world a better place. Working together, individuals within the group can complete many activities that will improve conditions in the community. These activities might include adopting a nonprofit organization to support and/or discuss issues and current events to help individuals clarify their position in order to take action such as in voting or volunteering. Working together, groups can make constructive changes in a community while building camaraderie among members. Group leaders should also encourage individuals to take part in organizations outside the group on their own such as volunteering with service organizations, religious institutions, and other civic-minded associations.

REFLECTION AND APPLICATION

REFLECTION AND APPLICATION

There are many other lists of character traits and values but we believe the ten included here are critical for a leader to succeed within his or her family or organization.

Take some time to look over the list of personal character traits and values. Which of these traits and values do you believe you are strong in?

_____

_____

_____

_____

_____

_____

_____

_____

Which do you need to work harder on?

_____

_____

_____

_____

_____

_____

_____

_____

_____

_____

Are there other traits and values you believe must be included as part of such a list? What are they and why do you believe they should be included?

_____

_____

_____

_____

_____

_____

_____

_____

_____

_____

_____

_____

_____

_____

_____

_____

_____

_____

_____

Emphasizing good character at work and at home can improve morale while increasing the effectiveness of the group. The next step in developing leadership is to look at ways to develop good character because just like the competency areas, character is something that can be developed through concentrated efforts carried out within a healthy and focused environment.

> **Good character is more to be praised than outstanding talent. Most talents are, to some extent, a gift. Good character, by contrast, is not given to us. We have to build it piece by piece—by thought, choice, courage and determination.**
>
> *— John Luther*

Creating an Environment for Effective Character Development

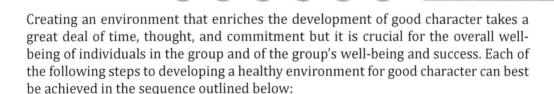

Creating an environment that enriches the development of good character takes a great deal of time, thought, and commitment but it is crucial for the overall well-being of individuals in the group and of the group's well-being and success. Each of the following steps to developing a healthy environment for good character can best be achieved in the sequence outlined below:

- *Assessment and Commitment.* Family and organizational leaders need to study the list of character traits and values that were enumerated earlier. Following your personal reflection and discussion with other group members about the list, make modifications to the list if deemed appropriate. It is important that this is a *shared vision* of traits and values for everyone to accept the list more readily. For practical purposes, try and keep the list to between ten and fifteen areas at most. Once you have completed an agreed-upon list of character traits and values, you should perform a self-assessment with each item on the list you have accepted as critical for good character. It is very common to feel strong in some areas and understand that work will be required in other areas.

Make a commitment to do just that; to work hard to be fully dedicated to the traits and values that you and your group have deemed necessary and even critical for success. Remember, actions speak louder than words. Live your life committed to your group and your shared values. Express yourself with integrity and determination. Let group members know that you genuinely care about them. Group members following leaders with strong character have a much easier time displaying good character themselves.

- *Preparing Others for Character Enrichment.* Once the list of traits and values is established and group members are determined to follow the guidelines of specific traits and values, then it is time to begin the work of adopting and enhancing these traits and characteristics. Each member of the group needs to understand why these traits and values are essential for success before they will be adopted and practiced. Formal and informal strategies can be implemented with leaders explaining the purpose of the activities and how the traits and values will be incorporated into the fabric of the group. Change is not always easy and often takes courage, determination, and patience before results can be appreciated. Anticipate setbacks and plan to work with the group to overcome barriers and promote change.

- *Encourage Others Toward Success.* Change is not easy, especially when there is a significant difference between new ways of operating and the way something has been done in the past. Most people get into routines and habits and need to break out of those routines and form new habits if they want to improve. Rewarding others for expressing their commitment and belief in the traits and values the group has selected is an important factor in promoting change. Praise, pats on the back, and celebrations of all kinds should be employed to reward individuals and teams for demonstrating strong character in the same manner that other achievements are acknowledged.

- *Model Good Character.* Unfortunately, there are a number of leaders who too often adopt the old adage "do as I say, not as I do." No one expects any member of a group to exemplify traits and values without exception, but it is very important that group leaders make every attempt to behave within the parameters of the character traits and values agreed upon as defining parameters for the group. At times, it might seem as though an added burden has been placed on leadership, but it is a responsibility that is well worth the results. It is much easier for group members to immerse themselves in the guidelines of good character when they experience family and organizational leaders behaving in accordance with the agreed-upon character traits and values. This requires patience and lots of practice doing what is clearly right as a wide variety of situations are encountered.

- *Review and Amend the Character Development Process as Needed.* Like any process in a family or organization, the process of character development should be reviewed from time to time to be certain that individuals continue to understand the importance of remaining true to the traits and values that the group has adopted. Leaders and members might be having a more difficult time adapting to particular traits or values. If those traits or values remain important to the group, discussions should be planned to help the group work through those difficulties. Also, other traits and values may need to be added from time to time if the review process suggests that this might help. As with the original list, it is much easier to adopt new traits or values if each person has some say in the decision-making process.

Just as character is the backbone of who an individual is, it can and should be the backbone of what a family or organization represents. Character development for individuals and groups is critical for the foundation of success. Leading with character means leading with the traits and values that you genuinely believe in and making a positive difference in the lives of those you interact with.

While character is critical for success it is also important to have a clear *purpose* for any family or organization and a strong *passion* for that purpose. The next step is to look at the importance that purpose plays in the success of a group.

Purpose Provides a Clear Direction for Success

While most businesses and community-based organizations have a formal mission statement or statement of purpose, most families have an unwritten, sometimes unclear mission. Whether written or informally understood, every type of organization should review their mission statements or understanding of purpose for clarity and reaffirmation.

A clear and strong purpose serves as a beacon of light that helps to guide, govern, and inspire group members toward the goals of the organization (Covey 1991). Understanding the purpose of a group and feeling essential to the achievement of that

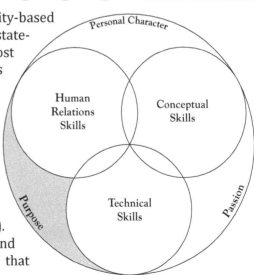

reason for existing as a group makes all the difference in the world. Group members who feel like they are an important part of the purpose and stay focused toward the objective have much higher morale and commitment level to the family or organization.

A purpose or mission statement is a vision of what a group hopes to achieve and should include the overall goals that the group is striving to accomplish as well as some of the core values such as the ones described earlier in this book. Including those agreed-upon goals and values in a statement of purpose allows the group to strive for what they hope to accomplish while maintaining the values they have set for themselves. In order for mission statements to provide direction, they should include a goal, a method of achieving that goal, and a measure of success (Tracy and Chee 2013, 31). For a business, the mission statement might include statements about creating the highest quality products while maintaining great customer service. Schools, charities, and nonprofit groups should create mission statements that identify the purpose of the organization and serve as a building block for marketing and branding.

Mission statements can identify the importance of teamwork, open communication, and integrity in the development of high quality products, or focus on the organization's commitment to the professional development of each employee and commitment to civic responsibilities through financial and volunteer opportunities. Youth and human service organizations such as Rotary International, the Lions Clubs, Boys and Girls Clubs of America, NAACP, YMCA, and Women's Clubs also include their goals and values with their statement of purpose. Evidence of the importance placed upon a well-written mission statement is seen in the placement of this message in the forefront of organizational publications. For example, if you go to the home page of almost any business or organization you will usually find their purpose or mission statement on the very first page.

For a family, the statement of purpose should also concentrate on the values and goals that they are focused on. Caring and commitment for one another and for members of the community, the importance of integrity, trust, love, communication, and the promise to help each family member become the best person they can become are all important considerations for a family's statement of purpose.

A statement of purpose should be broad enough that it encompasses important goals and values and should not be limiting in its scope. At the same time, it needs to be specific enough that individuals have a clear understanding of what the group's mission or purpose is focused on.

Leaders in any organization should strive for a *shared purpose* for their group which involves getting as much input from group members as possible. For a statement of purpose to be valued by everyone, each person should express their thoughts. Providing opportunities for individuals to freely express their thoughts on the purpose statement allows group members to get to know and develop a better appreciation for one another. The statement of purpose needs to be shared with prospective and new employees or members of a group, so that these individuals can decide if they are comfortable with the mission. A purpose statement should be inclusive but brief enough to easily identify and remember. Purpose statements can usually be articulated in several sentences, a paragraph or two, and might occasionally require a page or two. This should provide sufficient space to be inclusive while keeping it succinct enough to be effective.

Once activities begin, it is sometimes difficult to remain *focused* on the mission. There are lots of distractions and hurdles to overcome while attempting to accomplish various goals and objectives and remaining connected to the mission. The following is a list of steps for leaders to refer to for helping group members stay focused on the purpose of their family and/or organizations:

- *Develop a Shared and Effective Statement of Purpose.* Some of the best organizations in the world are considered the best in their field because they ask their members and customers (for businesses) for input on the content of the purpose statement. Getting input from all stakeholders can provide valuable information while at the same time allowing group members to feel like an integral part of the process. After requesting input from those involved, set times for discussion of the various ideas. Make drafts of the proposed statement of purpose and share them with those involved.

   Before preparing a final draft, be sure to include all the people who are a part of the organization and the constituents involved in developing the goals and values of the group. Make sure the statement is comprehensive enough to cover the most important aspects of the mission, specific enough to be clearly understood, yet brief enough to be easily followed. A good purpose statement is something that individuals will be attracted to, believe in, and feel fortunate to be involved.

- *Share your Purpose.* Once a statement of purpose is completed, it needs to be communicated with those associated with the organization. Concentrate first on group members and then on anyone else associated with the group that you believe needs to know about the agreed-upon purpose. This process varies considerably depending on whether the group is a family, a business, a nonprofit, or community organization. A summarized version of the purpose statement can be written on letterhead and posted throughout the home, business, or organization in places where constituents spend time. It can also be posted on the organization's website. Many organizations require individuals to go through training and ensure that part of the training involves understanding the purpose statement and its importance to the success of the group. The organization should continue to emphasize their purpose as appropriate, utilizing different strategies and activities.

- *Reinforce Members for Incorporating the Group's Purpose.* Members who make the purpose of the group a significant part of their culture should be acknowledged and commended for living with the goals and values of the organization. According to leadership experts, what gets rewarded is what gets done. Therefore, the reward structure should be tied to the goals of the organization (Tracy and Chee 2013, 132). Acknowledgments might include pats on the back, verbal praise, dinners out, awards, bonuses, raises, higher allowances, group celebrations, or other things that leaders might consider to emphasize the importance of living with the culture established, in part, by the statement of purpose. Simply following an organizational purpose that you genuinely believe in can be motivating in and of itself.

- *Model Your Purpose.* Just like other areas of leadership, when leaders' behaviors model and are closely aligned with the values and goals associated with the purpose statement it adds a great sense of legitimacy to the mission and provides a high level of inspiration for group members. For example, if concern for group members and community involvement is part of a group's mission, then emphasizing the importance of expressing your concern for the well-being of group members, and becoming involved in community service activities become important ways of letting others know that the organization's purpose statement is more than just a saying; it is a concept you believe in and emulate throughout your life.

  The idea of leading by example has been shown to result in better outcomes for an organization. Research has revealed that reciprocally-oriented leaders contribute more than selfish leaders to achieving the group's goals (Gächter, Nosenzo, Renner, and Sefton 2012). Leading by example is one of the strongest things you can do to ensure that the statement of purpose is not just a bunch of words printed for effect, with little substance.

- *Monitor Activities Surrounding the Purpose Statement.* Like most things in life, the needs of families, businesses, and other organizations change over time. Families might need to consider change to meet the demand of a busier and faster paced culture or consider the best way to succeed within a busier culture; businesses often change to meet the requirements of the area(s) of commerce they are involved with, while other organizations often change according to the needs of those associated with the organization. In this sense, leaders need to keep a careful watch to be sure that the goals and values group members originally set as their purpose continue to be valid and effective for those concerned.

  There is a need to monitor the communication process to be certain that the group's purpose is shared frequently, clearly, thoroughly, and effectively. It is also prudent to ensure that individuals who are intimately involved with the function of the organization are encouraged and reinforced for their efforts and that all contributions to this end are celebrated appropriately.

Living your personal life within the context of the purpose statement is critical in inspiring and providing a living guide for others. "Walk the talk" as they say, to demonstrate to everyone that the statement of purpose of the organization is a lot more than just a neat phrase to be hung on a wall and forgotten.

A clear, strong, and effective statement of purpose is crucial to maintaining a high level of energy toward what a group hopes to accomplish and includes the values that are associated with activities designed toward meeting goals.

REFLECTION AND APPLICATION

A clear, strong, and effective statement of purpose is crucial to maintaining a high level of energy toward what a group hopes to accomplish and includes the values that are associated with activities designed toward meeting goals.

When was the last time you participated in a discussion of purpose with regard to your work or family? What was the outcome of that discussion?

_____

_____

_____

_____

_____

_____

_____

_____

_____

After reviewing the list of five steps to improving purpose (mentioned above), how can you improve your purpose at work and at home?

_____

_____

_____

_____

_____

_____

_____

_____

_____

What are some ways to promote your purpose to others?

_____

_____

_____

_____

_____

_____

_____

_____

_____

Remaining focused on the group's purpose is as important as identifying and promoting the group's principles. Over time, striving toward the organization's goals and other aspects can become tiring or frustrating. Success in any organization can become stagnant or even decline over time because leadership becomes stale and tired. Therefore, we will outline ways to develop and keep passion toward the overall purpose of the organization and in other areas of your life.

Passion Keeps the Spark of Success Glowing

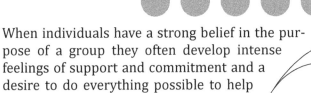

When individuals have a strong belief in the purpose of a group they often develop intense feelings of support and commitment and a desire to do everything possible to help realize their mutual goals and aspirations. *Passion* is created; it is not some magical feeling that just happens. Angela Maiers, lead consultant at Maiers' Educational Services, makes the following statement about the importance of passion in our leaders. "We are impacted by those who we spend time with. I am energized . . . when I am surrounded by passionate people." (2009) Maiers explains that the opposite is also true. Individuals who are unmotivated can drain the energy and productivity from those around them.

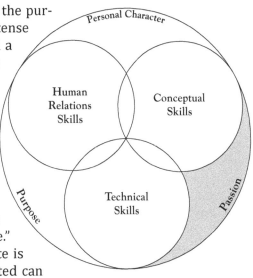

Individuals must have a conviction for the purpose of a group and work consistently and diligently toward that end in spite of the hurdles experienced along the way. Group members must share a passion for their goals to succeed. It is up to leadership within families, businesses, and other organizations to help members develop and maintain the passion that is necessary to be great.

We may affirm absolutely that nothing great in the world has been accomplished without passion.

— Hegel

The consistency and intensity of passion is often contagious especially when that passion is communicated consistently and appropriately. Emotion can be communicated through quiet determination or through zealous enthusiasm, regardless of the display a real sense of conviction needs to be conveyed. Passion can and should be expressed through commitment to the group's values, goals, and purpose to individuals through genuine concern, support, and loyalty. Passion can also be expressed through the confidence that leadership has in the objectives of the group and in the character and abilities of individual group members.

Developing and sustaining passion for the purpose of a group is critical so that members will continue to feel excited and fulfilled as they go about day-to-day tasks, activities, and responsibilities. The following is a list of suggested steps that leaders can take to foster the development of passion in group members for the desired outcomes:

- *Lead by Example/Share your Passion with Others.* It's important to share your enthusiasm for the purpose of the group with all stakeholders. One way to do this is by emphasizing, through words and actions, the significance of the overall goals of the group. Passionate leaders often work alongside group members championing their efforts and letting others know the importance of their contributions. Even through difficult times, passionate leaders remain focused on the purpose of the group and their words and actions support that commitment. When others sense that passion it helps substantiate the group's purpose and helps others grow in their own dedication. Passion is contagious and transformational and sharing a common devotion is one of the greatest feelings group members can experience.

A man without passion is a fire without a light.

— Chuck Gallozzi

- *Live and Lead in the Present.* Another important way to develop passion in oneself and in others is to realize the importance of living and leading in the present. Bestselling author Wayne Dyer writes about the tendency most of us have of spending a good portion of our time thinking about the future or ruminating over the past (2012). We owe it to ourselves, our family, and to the organizations we are a part of to make the most of the present moment. The past is important and we can use those experiences to provide us with confidence and direction but some past experiences can be harsh and can become hurdles for success in the present and in the future and so they need to be put into perspective.

Sarah's Story

There is a story about a mother and her young daughter that helps put things in perspective. The mother had been betrayed by the child's dad who, after fathering the child denied his involvement in parenthood and actually left the area, never to be heard from again. The mother worked hard and sacrificed often for her daughter's sake and eventually became a model citizen, working in a bank, first as a teller then later as a vice president. All the while, letting the little girl know how much she was loved and how special she was. The mother taught the little girl how to care for others by letting her volunteer with her at the local Red Cross Chapter and in their church. The mother led with passion and didn't let the past enslave her or her daughter. She lived in the present, using the past as a marker, and the future as something to look forward to.

To put it another way, the past is over, but how we choose to use it, learn from it, or let it harm us is a choice we must make. It is also important to use the present to plan and prepare for the future and remember that much of what happens tomorrow is influenced by what we think, feel, and do today, it is what we do in the present that enables us to achieve our wishes and aspirations. Realizing the importance of *now* provides a renewed sense of energy and purpose that must be shared with those around us.

The future is not something we enter.
The future is something we create.

— Leonard J. Sweet

- *Create an Open and Welcoming Environment.* Most of us can better express our passion for things when we feel that the emotions associated with this expression are encouraged and welcomed. Encouraging group members to share ideas, suggestions, and concerns helps others develop confidence in offering their thoughts. When those ideas can be acted upon, it considerably increases the likelihood of additional ideas being offered. Many organizations and businesses have increased their market share significantly by conducting surveys and focus groups to ask constituents and customers what they think about the services or products being offered. If the results are used to enhance the quality of what is being offered, it has the potential to dramatically impact the organization in a positive way. This same concept can and should be used with staff members, volunteers, and members of organizations, as well as family members. It is also important to create activities that are fun to do in safe, cheerful, and comfortable surroundings when possible; this adds interest and excitement to tasks and helps create the feeling of being a part of something wonderful (Boverie and Kroth 2005).

- *Invite Input for Individual and Team Responsibilities.* Identifying responsibilities and tasks to be addressed can become so much easier to accomplish when the individuals involved have input as to the specific details of their assigned responsibilities. When individuals like and value their responsibilities, they spend more time enjoying what they are doing and are more committed to quality and to their job (Peck 1978.) Finding out what others really like to do, in conjunction with what needs to be done, takes time on the part of the leader but it is time very well spent.

  In their book, *Transforming Work: The Five Keys to Achieving Trust, Commitment, and Passion in the Workplace,* authors Boverie and Kroth (2001) state that one of the four major pitfalls that detracts from a passionate group environment is working in an overly controlled setting in which you have very little autonomy. People feel complemented when asked to share input on individual and team responsibilities, groups benefit from a broader range of information and stronger bonds develop between leader and group members. Stronger bonds lead to an improved sense of group accomplishment.

One person with passion is better than forty people merely interested.

—E.M. Forster

- *Design Tasks That are Challenging and Meaningful.* Working on tasks that are significant to the overall purpose of a group and understanding the importance of specific tasks are keys to feeling that what an individual is doing has meaning. Recognizing that what we do is making a difference in the lives of others and developing confidence in overcoming the challenges in completing tasks also helps our passion grow. Leaders are charged with designing tasks for group members that provide a sense of meaning and that members understand and embrace that meaning. Allowing others to have a say in identifying aspects of their assigned tasks increases the meaningfulness of their work. Meaningful participation has been identified as a key component to increasing resiliency within individuals (Benard 2002).

In contrast, when individuals find work boring and mundane, any potential passion is dissipated leading them to opt out of the group if possible. Non-meaningful work can play a large role when individuals do not connect with a particular group. Recognizing the significance of work helps people feel good about what they are doing. When they understand how important their success is in their lives and in the lives of others, they are more likely to be excited and motivated and feel proud of their accomplishments (Boverie and Kroth 2001).

When people are doing what they love to do, time seems to fly by. Successfully completing tasks in areas in which they feel a connection helps to build confidence and an even stronger commitment. Identities merge with these accomplishments and a true sense of self-efficacy and pride develops.

- *Supervise with Empowerment.* Leaders are also charged with the challenge of matching individuals or small groups with the appropriate tasks and with monitoring progress in order to make adjustments whenever necessary. Leaders also need to make sure that members are provided sufficient support to enable them to complete tasks successfully and on schedule. Good training, demonstrations, modeling, providing examples, encouragement, and monitoring progress are all important ways to ensure that others are successful with tasks. Once individuals gain experience with specific duties, providing them with opportunities to lead and have influence is *empowering*. When individuals feel empowered, they are encouraged to use initiative and are able to work more competently and confidently (Weis and Gantt 2009). Individuals and teams who are encouraged to work on tasks with a certain degree of autonomy and freedom will often develop a deep passion for their activities (Bennis and Townsend 1995).

  Empowerment is a significant aspect of leadership and will be discussed again in another section.

- *Encourage, Recognize, and Celebrate Others for their Efforts.* The importance of acknowledging and appreciating others for their efforts in support of the purpose of the group cannot be overstated. While relationships between group members are important, one of the most important relationships is between group members and their leaders. Leaders must be seen as people of influence who can be trusted to employ their knowledge and skills and to behave with character, which leads to respect.

  Being recognized or encouraged by a respected leader for doing well is one of the most motivating processes that can occur, increasing desire to help achieve the group's goals. Recognition can come in many forms, the best form being the one that that specific group member prefers. Examples include a kind and grateful word, a pat on the back, a note, a promotion, public acknowledgment, or other ways the organization has identified to recognize deserving individuals. Groups can also host parties and dinners to celebrate the collective accomplishments of their members. Passionate individuals identify with their group and its purpose and need to be encouraged to do their very best to increase the chances for success. Leaders who guide and support individuals and work beside them in their efforts through good and difficult times, create a transformational culture for individuals to achieve increasing levels of success and a strong sense of belonging and accomplishment.

People will forget what you said, people will forget what you did, but people will never forget how you made them feel.

— Maya Angelou

Passionate individuals have a strong belief in the group's purpose and they are committed to achieving success despite facing obstacles along the way. Members who share this enthusiasm for the group's intentions are more likely to work smoothly and effectively in accomplishing the established goals. Group leaders must be willing and able to share their emotion and empower others to be consistently and highly passionate in their efforts toward the mission.

REFLECTION AND APPLICATION

How passionate do you think you are for your group's purpose?

_____

_____

_____

_____

_____

_____

_____

_____

_____

_____

_____

How would you describe the passion level of others in your group?

_____

_____

_____

_____

_____

_____

_____

_____

_____

_____

_____

_____

_____

What are some of the things you can do to elevate levels of passion for your group's purpose?

_____

_____

_____

_____

_____

_____

_____

How can you raise the passion level in your family?

_____

_____

_____

_____

_____

_____

_____

While character, purpose, and passion are critical for successful leadership, it is just as important to have skills in competency areas. Next, we will look at the interrelated competency areas that enhance strong leadership.

Developing Interrelated Competencies

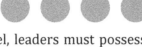

According to the model, leaders must possess or develop an effective level of conceptual, technical, and human relation skills to be successful, or be able to collaborate with those who are competent in these three competency areas. Let us examine these competency areas, describe how these competencies can be developed, and illustrate how they might be integrated into leadership at home and work.

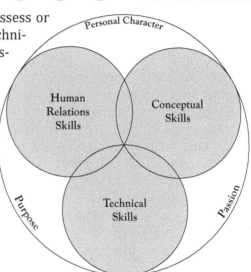

If one advances confidently in the direction of his dreams, and endeavors to live the life which he has imagined, he will meet with a success unexpected in common hours.

— Henry David Thoreau

Understanding and Developing Conceptual Competencies

Conceptual skills or *competencies* are usually associated with critical thinking and include: vision, decision making, and problem solving. A conceptual competency is, in effect, a theoretical capability. Despite that, there are substantive processes designed to develop conceptual attributes.

Vision Serves to Focus and Inspire

"Where there is no vision, the people perish" Prov.29:18 (KJV). This bold and clear statement strongly implies that organizations and families need a direction to focus their resources and attention.
In 1989, Stephen Covey wrote *The 7 Habits of Highly Effective People* and habit #2 was, *Begin with the End in Mind.* In effect, Covey was saying that individuals need to envision the end of whatever process is being considered. Whether it is their life, an entire career, or simply a single project, individuals must ask how they would like to be remembered; as a person, an organizational member, or as a community member?

Covey suggests there are two steps in visioning. The first step involves a mental picture while the second stage is more physical. The mental picture includes a mental image regarding what a family or organization is about, where each unit needs to be headed, and a plan that could make the vision a reality. This might be likened to a contractor working with a blueprint. Before the foundation can be set and the walls can begin to go up, there needs to be a blueprint that includes these two aspects of the plan along with many other details.

Covey wrote that you need to begin every day, every relationship, and every activity envisioning what you hope that scenario will become, followed by planning and acting according to this plan. Similar to building a house with a blueprint, the structure might change from the original design, only if the parties agree to change or if there is an error during implementation. Covey went on to state that individuals should develop a *principle centered vision*, in which the vision is based, in part, on the principles and values that guide their life. This image should be a *shared vision* in which we invite family members, organizational members, and community members to offer input.

According to Senge (1990), "A vision is truly shared when you and I have a similar picture and are committed to one another having it, not just to each of us, individually, having it. When people truly share a vision, they are connected, bound together by a common inspiration" (206). So not only does a shared vision provide a focus but it is also motivational in that members become excited about working toward the same goals. Incorporating aspects of the *invitational leadership* model and the *servant leadership* model could also be helpful in developing a shared vision because both philosophies encourage active involvement of individuals in the leadership process.

One of the most respected authors of our time on the subject of leadership is John Maxwell who identified *vision* as a key quality of a leader in his book *The 21 Indispensable Qualities of a Leader (*1999). According to Maxwell, vision starts from within. Individuals need to be able to recognize their calling and sometimes partner with another person who shares this vision and possesses the aptitude to bring it to fruition. Maxwell went on to say that vision is not a mystical quality but rather is born from our experiences in the past. He states that vision is far-reaching and to be truly effective it must add value to the lives of others. Maxwell concluded with the idea that if the vision is clear and appealing and communicated thusly, it will attract and unite people. Individuals must feel good about taking part in the realization of a family or organization's vision. Sharing helps develop a collaborative commitment toward mutual goals and the development of a group's *purpose* as previously discussed.

Developing a shared vision with others can be as simple as collecting and assessing ideas and information. Round-table discussions at home, business lunches at work, interviews, or surveys with constituents; all contribute to the knowledge base serving to inform the vision of a group. Usually the ideas are already pretty much there; they just have to be requested, assimilated, and followed by open and flexible discussions regarding the direction that the group wishes to take. The direction or vision might need to be re-tooled at times, depending on changing needs and circumstances.

A good example of this process occurred when the Scandinavian Airline System (SAS) began to rework their vision and mission statement back in the mid-1990s. They started the process by surveying their business class customers. Business travelers fly quite a bit more than most others and they usually are able to afford higher fares. SAS assimilated the information they found and actually implemented programs and amenities based on the surveys resulting in unparalleled success (Kotter 1990).

One important thing to keep in mind is to value the ideas of others and treat each idea as if it might become a part of the overall vision of the group. Stephen Covey's 5th habit was *Seek First to Understand, Then to Be Understood* (1989) in which he describes the importance of genuinely listening and trying to understand the thoughts and feelings of others prior to developing an overall vision. If others perceive you as having a real interest in their opinions, a trusting relationship might ensue and ideas can really start flowing.

When individuals share a vision and a desire, have effective tools, knowledge, and enthusiasm, there is almost nothing they cannot accomplish.

REFLECTION AND APPLICATION

Make it a point to sit down with family and work team members and discuss the vision of your family or the work group. Is it a shared vision and how so?

_____

_____

_____

_____

_____

_____

_____

_____

_____

_____

_____

How does your current vision at home or work guide what you do as a group?

_____

_____

_____

_____

_____

_____

_____

_____

_____

_____

_____

Does it need revision? If so, what is your plan for revision?

_____

_____

_____

_____

_____

_____

_____

_____

_____

_____

_____

Effective Decision Making
Leads Us Toward Success

Making the right decisions in various matters is just as important as having an enlightened and strong vision. *Decision making* is important, time consuming, and often complicated for families and for organizations. Reaching appropriate decisions can make all the difference in the world in moving toward success.

Because decision making is so important there are five tenets recommended for consideration prior to getting involved with a decision-making process:

1. As with vision, make important decisions, *principle-centered decisions.* Principle-centered decisions are those that are made with the values of the family or organization in mind as ideas and alternatives are considered. Values such as *respect, responsibility*, *fairness*, and *integrity* should always be taken into account when making important decisions.

    Respecting individuals who may be involved in a decision-making process and those who may be affected by the process is critical to leading with character. Realizing and accepting responsibility for each decision made provides added incentive to make the best decisions possible. Maintaining fairness for all of those involved in the consequences of our decisions can be challenging, but it needs to be an essential component of the process. Finally, everyone needs to be able to trust that we are making the best decisions possible and that our level of integrity is high.

It's not hard to make decisions when you know
what your values are.

— Roy Disney

---

2. Concentrate on the big picture, keeping the *purpose* of the family or organization in mind when making significant decisions. For instance, sometimes one decision might seem to be in conflict with another. Review of the vision of the family or organization might help to clarify which of the conflicting decisions serves the best interests of the group. Frequent review of the vision

increases the chance of decisions being made according to the overall goals of the group.

Keep in mind that the vision or purpose of a group can change depending on shifting needs and circumstances. Therefore, it is also important to revisit the vision to be sure that everyone is on the same page and that decisions are based on a common understanding of the overall purpose of the group.

3. *Invite* as many individuals to be a part of the decision-making process as is possible and realistic. Inviting others to be a part of the process when making important decisions provides more input and energy and gives each person a sense that they are a valued member of the team. Involving others is often a *transformational* process because individuals are interacting and developing a synergy that changes the group's dynamic. This transformation usually helps the group make healthy, enlightened decisions. It is certainly an *invitational* process in that respect and caring are demonstrated when inviting others to the table. Involving others in the decision-making process is also a component of *servant leadership,* because the leader is asking others what they are hoping for in the decision-making process.

    Decision making that includes more of those individuals with a stake in the outcome has a much better chance of yielding results that are seen as *win-win.* When everyone feels represented in the overall process, there is less chance that the position of any single constituency will be neglected. According to Mark Ryckman, of Demand Media, there are several key benefits of including stakeholders in the decision-making process. Stakeholders have unique insight into issues; can help secure resources to assist in making decisions on the project; can build trust, increase transparency, and lead to increased consensus for the final decision. Inviting the appropriate representatives for all stakeholders to the decision-making process takes intelligence, insight, and sometimes even courage, but the results can go a long way in establishing a foundation of trust, involvement, and success.

4. *Emotion* is invariably a part of the decision-making process and it should not be taken lightly. Scientists have an ongoing debate about involving emotions during the decision-making process and whether this is functional or maladaptive (Gohm and Clore 2002). Seo and Barrett (2007) suggest that the answer is largely dependent upon how people experience those feelings and what they do about them during the decision-making process. These authors propose that individuals are able to experience intense emotions during decision making and at the same time regulate the possible biases induced by those feelings, adding that both of these occurrences might positively contribute to the decision-making performance.

Understanding the emotions that individuals bring to the process and determining whether these are passion born out of significant insight and knowledge or represent strong, personal desires is essential. If someone has a high level of passion derived from his or her expertise, insight and knowledge for a particular direction he/she wishes the group to move toward, then that should be taken into consideration. However, if these emotions appear to be based mostly on personal needs or desires then this input probably should not be as carefully considered.

5. *Leadership* style plays a significant part in determining how decisions are to be made and how successful the results will be. There might be a question about whether or when a leader should make a decision independently of a group or if and when group members should be involved. Research suggests that letting entire groups make decisions takes more time and energy, but the decisions are more readily accepted and the results of the decisions will be implemented more effectively (Vroom 1995). When comparing decisions made by a group process to those made by an individual, the following observations have been made. One is that shifts in the decision of groups tend to occur in the direction of the original inclination of the group, or toward the inclination of the majority. The second observation is that decision shifts are less likely to occur when groups tend to have fairly equal number of people predisposed one way versus the other described as a symmetrical distribution.

Some decisions require a quicker turnaround or may best be left in the hands of a few and these decisions can also be effective if evaluated and implemented carefully. Anecdotal evidence suggests that a leader who is often inviting and democratic will be more likely to have a decision-making process that is well-received and implemented and more likely to have group members feel as though they are part of the overall team.

The tenets outlined above provide a good foundation of thought prior to the actual decision-making process encouraging us to reflect on important considerations that add quality to the overall process. Most experts in the area of leadership and decision making promote a step-by-step process. Depending on the expert, the steps could range anywhere from three to twenty or more in number. One concept promoted by management editor, consultant, and university president, E. Frank Harrison, includes a six-step process that is simple, yet profound, in its potential (1983). Remember to review the tenets prior to using the decision-making process developed by Harrison and to fold those tenets into the process when appropriate.

1. *Setting objectives.* A family or organizational group must first agree on their objectives (*purpose*) and the more involved individuals are

in the setting of objectives the more likely they are to believe in those objectives and to work hard toward achieving them.

2. *Searching for alternatives.* This part of the decision-making process calls for thorough searches for information relating to the objectives that are being considered. Searching for information internally with the group should be a priority but researching information externally can also prove to be valuable. Once all of the information is assimilated, group members can suggest possible alternatives in making a decision.

3. *Comparing and evaluating alternatives.* All reasonable alternatives should be considered. Each alternative or potential choice must be evaluated alone or in combination based on anticipated outcomes and consequences. Anticipated outcomes should not only focus on the objectives of the group but should also align with the group's values.

4. *The act of choice.* This is one of the most challenging parts to making a decision, determining which alternative will have the best outcome. Experience, history, knowledge, and teamwork should also play into the process of making a decision from a number of alternatives.

5. *Implementing the decision.* Once a decision has been reached, it is necessary to take steps to put the decision into effect. This moves the choice from a concept to an operational process. Each person involved in the decision-making process should be aware of when and how the decision is to be implemented.

6. *Follow-up and monitoring.* The implementation of a decision needs to be monitored throughout this entire stage to ensure that it is employed as intended and is meeting the intended objective(s). Some decisions will need to be fine-tuned or changed altogether during the operational process. It is important for a leader to recognize when change is necessary and to discuss these modifications with others.

REFLECTION AND APPLICATION
REFLECTION AND APPLICATION

Making the right kinds of decisions is crucial to having successful groups.

_____

_____

_____

_____

_____

_____

_____

_____

_____

_____

_____

Have your decisions in the past been *principle-centered* decisions? Explain.

_____

_____

_____

_____

_____

_____

_____

_____

_____

_____

_____

How can you incorporate more *principle-centered* decisions into your future decision-making process?

_____

_____

_____

_____

_____

_____

_____

Would you like to invite more individuals to the decision-making process? Who should they be?

_____

_____

_____

_____

_____

_____

_____

Which of the concepts on decision making can be most helpful to you, now or in the future?

_____

_____

_____

_____

_____

_____

_____

Solving Problems with Others

Problems in any family or organization are inevitable and there are as many ways to solve problems as there are ways to make good, strong decisions. We would like to guide you toward some of the more reliable and verified problem-solving techniques and ways to solve problems as a team. Since problems are inevitable, the more effective a group is in solving problems the stronger their bonds and the more successful the family or organization will become.

Working through problems often establishes developmental cornerstones for individuals and groups. Although sometimes appealing, a life of least resistance often leads to a life without challenge or opportunities to develop character, strength, stamina, and determination. Lack of challenge or opposition can lead to groups of individuals without real testing and therefore without bonding, camaraderie, and success.

Often, the things that challenge us in life become the things that help make us who we are. For example, Hellen Keller was challenged by unbelievable disabilities but worked through them with the help of Anne Sullivan to become a leader and mentor to thousands of others with disabilities. Martin Luther King, Jr. was challenged by a system of racism and injustice but worked through it with the help of like-minded individuals to become the iconic figure of someone striving for justice and fairness for all.

All three of these individuals had the same thing in common; they each faced unbelievably challenging situations yet instead of giving up and running away or hiding from them they faced them head-on, developed a plan to meet the challenge, and worked with others who had similar goals. The results of facing challenges head-on, with a strong plan and a great team can be unbelievable.

Developing a good structure and a great team is the idea behind the three-step plan for avoiding and/or managing problems.

1. *Be Proactive.* Recognizing situations that have the potential to become problematic and addressing the situation before problems actually occur is often the best course of action. By remaining cognizant of potential results, good leaders develop a sense of possible and sometimes probable consequences of their actions. One way to heighten the sense of awareness is by involving others in assessing various scenarios and determining potential hazards. Effective leaders keep an open mind; they encourage others to participate in the review of potential downfalls even when the opinions expressed run counter to popular ways of thinking. They hold meetings to discuss concerns and try to prevent potentially negative outcomes.

Establishing preventative safeguards for procedures and activities can be a very effective way to head problems off at the pass. Try to involve as many people as possible in establishing policies and procedures to safeguard the group. The more family and organizational members are involved in establishing ways to prevent problems, the stronger they will feel about the safeguards and the more likely they will be to follow them.

2. *Think Outside the Box.* Many problems can be addressed with tried and proven processes that have worked in the past or through a similar process. However, not every problem can be solved in predictable ways. Sometimes it takes stretching the imagination and taking chances; trying things that seem different but may have the potential to address certain situations. Almost every family, business, or organization will have to try something different and new to work some of their unique problems out. Leonardo da Vinci was far from an ordinary thinker, to say the least, and he established several principles to consider when working on problems (Gelb 1998):

   • Maintain a strong and curious approach to life and never allow yourself to stop learning.
   • Remain open to test your thoughts through experience and be willing to learn from mistakes.
   • Keep your senses alive in order to fully experience, appreciate, and learn from life.
   • Don't shy away from uncertainty and paradox; some of life's greatest discoveries occur through assessing all possibilities.
   • Try to have a balance between artistic, creative endeavors and more logical, scientific endeavors in order to become a well-rounded individual.
   • In the face of adversity try to maintain a sense of grace, poise, and fitness.
   • Recognize and appreciate the interconnectedness of all things.

   Da Vinci was convinced that incorporating one or more of these principles in problem-solving situations could be very effective. Thinking outside the box, as da Vinci suggests, often leads to unusual responses to difficult problems, which may result in the best way to address certain situations.

3. *Use a Problem-Solving Process.* In addition to being proactive and stepping outside the box to manage problems, it is a very good idea to incorporate a proven process in problem-solving situations. The following process was developed in large part by Maxwell (1993) and provides guidelines for handling problem situations:

   • *Identify and Understand the Problem.* Some situations seem to plague us because we have not fully recognized or understood the significance of a problem. The devil really is in the details and we need to understand the parameters of a problem well before we can begin to address something adequately. Because each individual brings different insights, knowledge, and opinions to the table, it is imperative that individuals involved with a problem be invited to help identify the issue; to define its overall significance and its details.

Sitting down with family members, meeting with organizational or business colleagues, and expressing the idea that a problem may exist then developing a group mindset as to what the problem may be and its finer points is a major factor in working toward a solution or a way to manage the situation.

- *Prioritize the Problem.* Most families and organizations are juggling many balls at the same time resulting in problems appearing at inopportune times. Therefore, once a problem has been identified and understood by a group, it may need to be prioritized as to when it might be addressed. With some problems it is important to address the situation immediately; other problems may need more time for study or may not require the action necessitated by others. If a problem is relegated to a back burner, but it has been identified by a group as important, then it is imperative that a time period for addressing the problem be identified. It is essential that the situation is understood and that group members are kept abreast of the ongoing status of the problem.
- *Select Effective Team Members.* It is true; some problems can easily be managed alone. But if the problem is significant, it is important for a number of reasons to invite the appropriate individuals to be a part of the team. Individuals who are invited to be involved in the problem-solving process will feel as if they are valued. They will bring a variety of ideas to the table as to the causes of the problem(s) and ways to manage the situation. Once a solution is identified, they will be more enthusiastic about implementing the resolution.

Individuals who are affected by the problem or your solution should be considered as participants in the process in addition to group members with particular expertise. Personal character also needs to be considered when selecting people to help in the decision-making process. Consider whether they are able to combine reason with a passion to work on problem situations. As da Vinci would recommend, consider thinking outside the box when it comes to individuals who may help in certain situations.

- *Determine Causes and Problem-Solving Solutions.* With a team in place, you can begin to brainstorm ideas as to the overriding causes of the problem(s) being considered. In a brainstorming session, it is a good idea to let all opinions be heard and appraised before going over the list. Thorough research is encouraged so that no stone is left unturned.

Individuals outside the group can also be considered; consultants and problem-solving specialists should always be contemplated for a family or an organization if the problem is significant enough and requires different expertise.

Once the core of a problem is understood, it is time to encourage team members to explore as many ways to manage the problem as possible. Those ideas should be expressed and explained. The quick review of several ideas or brainstorming is a great way to put lots of ideas on the table without any large emotional investment in a specific solution. Leaders need to encourage team members to feel comfortable in making suggestions and ensure that no one's ideas are denigrated.

- *Prioritize, Select, and Implement the Most Effective Solution.* Careful and thorough research along with inviting the best team members to be part of a problem-solving process should lead to a list of strong, potential solutions. Maxwell (1993) suggests that the leader follow up on the idea-generating process by asking the following questions:

  ✓ Which solution has the greatest potential for effectiveness?
  ✓ Which solution will be most helpful for the family/organization?
  ✓ Which solution has momentum and feasibility?
  ✓ Which solution has the greatest chance to work?

Once there is general agreement among group members as to the most effective way to handle a problem, the next step is to develop a plan to implement the solution as soon as is reasonable. It is imperative that individuals of the group who are assigned action steps implement these measures to manage or solve a problem and that other members are kept informed.

- *Evaluate and Monitor the Solution.* Just because a solution to a problem has been identified, this does not necessarily mean that it will work as planned. Plus, variables associated with a problem can change at any moment so it is critical that the leader and team members keep a watchful eye on the progress of the solution and that adjustments are made if and when necessary. It is also important that enough time is devoted to a process to determine its worthiness. There is often a delicate balance involved in allowing enough time for solutions to work and understanding that adjustments are needed to achieve a successful outcome. Setting group meetings at specific junctures to measure progress is a great idea.

Solving problems with others not only provides opportunities for more ideas to be considered, but it also provides additional opportunities for bonding among team members. The process can help strengthen confidence in one another as individuals and in the group as a working body. Problems are inevitable; but like an old friend once said, "It is not the number of flat tires you have in life that matters, what is important is how well you fix them!"

Think back over the past few months and recent problems that your group has been confronted with and the methods that were used to manage these problems. Were these methods successful and can they be replicated in the future? The problem-solving processes discussed in this section might be helpful in the future.

The way I see it, if you want the rainbow you gotta put up with the rain.

— Dolly Parton

REFLECTION AND APPLICATION

What are some recent problems your group or family has had to address?

_____

_____

_____

_____

_____

_____

_____

_____

_____

_____

_____

_____

What methods were used to manage these problems?

_____

_____

_____

_____

_____

_____

_____

_____

_____

_____

_____

_____

Which methods were successfully employed, and can they be used in the future?

_____

_____

_____

_____

_____

_____

_____

_____

_____

_____

How can the problem-solving processes discussed in this section be helpful in the future?

_____

_____

_____

_____

_____

_____

_____

_____

_____

_____

_____

_____

Understanding and Developing Technical Competencies

Conceptual thinking is important in developing vision, decision-making, while problem solving and technical skills or competencies are the nuts, bolts, and tools that are crucial in putting the visions, decisions, and solutions together. Several technical competencies that are useful at home and work include planning, budgeting, stewardship, empowerment, and personal balance.

Personal Character

Human Relations Skills

Conceptual Skills

Purpose

Technical Skills

Passion

Planning with Skill and Purpose

There is an old saying that goes, "The best made plans of mice and men often go astray." Although this is sometimes true, effective planning can make all the difference in the world in the successes associated with any family or organization. Planning as a leadership skill requires that you nurture and cultivate your ability to build for a very unpredictable future. As Alvin Toffler, author of the best-selling book *Future Shock* notes, "You've got to think about big things while you're doing small things, so that all the small things go in the right direction." (1984) The quality of activities, projects, services, and products often indicate how effective family and organizational members are in the planning process. Effective planning involves asking family members, organizational members, and constituents what they hope for with certain activities, services, and products. A *People Centered/Benefits Approach* to planning implies that leaders strive to develop activities, projects, or products that not only meet the expectations of individuals involved but might even exceed them and provide a positive outcome (Weis and Gantt 2009). Quality activities, projects, and products must be carefully planned, implemented, and evaluated. Effective planning can include a step-by-step process although the sequence and number of steps may vary from one activity or project to another.

1. *Select a Planning Team.* Involving a number of different individuals on the planning team often results in greater creativity, synergy, and expertise.

Groups have greater possibilities for comprehensive planning than do individuals and should include:

- family and/or organizational members with specific expertise in the activity, project, or product area
- family members, organizational members, or constituents who are involved with or who stand to benefit from the activity, project, or product
- consultants or others with specific expertise in the area of interest

Planning committee members should be responsible for the following:

- develop a schedule for meetings
- identify and prioritize a sequence of planning steps
- assign individuals to coordinate each step
- implement, monitor, and adjust plans when necessary
- discuss and evaluate results

2. *Find out what People Need and Want.* Before planning activities, projects, or products it is smart to understand what individuals need or want. *Needs* are usually understood to be deficiencies in areas of physiological, psychological, or social imbalance. When an individual recognizes a deficiency in any of these areas, it is considered a need (Edginton and Ford 1985). Physiological needs can include food, water, sleep, or sex whereas psychological or social needs could include the need for companionship, recognition, social interaction, self–esteem, love, and achievements (Weis and Gantt 2009). *Desires,* which are considered wishes that are often perceived as needs, should also be considered in planning projects and products.

There is a grocery store in the northeastern part of the United States whose owners sit down with customers on an ongoing basis in a focus group setting and ask them what they think of current items and services, and what they might like in the way of new items or services. They implement as many of the suggestions from their customers as is reasonable. This attention to what their constituents want has resulted in increasing business significantly over the past several decades.

A needs assessment can help determine what family members believe is important regarding their daily lives and beyond. It can help determine if organizational members are feeling fulfilled in their roles and it can help determine what organizational constituents or customers value in the context of services and products.

There are at least two effective processes for determining needs and desires and both should be considered: (1) Leaders need to assess existing data that includes published reports in magazines, newspapers, journals, and other informational venues. (2) Assessing the needs and desires of family and organizational members and constituents firsthand can be done through informal and/or formal interviews, focus groups, and written surveys. Interviews and focus groups can provide lots of information and surveys gather data and also provide an opportunity to offer suggestions and ideas with some anonymity.

Many businesses have individuals and departments that conduct needs assessments or they work with consultants to find out what their constituents and/or employees are thinking. As the workplace evolves, employees are expected to learn new skills, improve acquired skills, and learn to be competent in many different areas. The push to increase efficiency might result in combining what used to be two jobs into one new position, regardless of the current individual's skill set. Rapid changes in technology have created a situation where it takes more effort to keep work-related skills up-to-date. It is now recommended that organizations conduct skills testing to see where their employees stand in reference to specific skill sets. This testing is one way to assess individual needs for professional development within an organization.

Family leaders can hold meetings from time to time to see what members are thinking. More information on conducting a needs assessment can be found by researching community resources through the Better Business Bureau, the United Way, or local colleges or universities. Information can also be found on conducting a needs assessment in the book, *Knowledge and Skill Development in Nonprofit Organizations* by Weis and Gantt (2004).

3. *Incorporate Values and Mission in the Planning Process.* Anytime a family or an organization is in the planning process, it is very important to consider the principles (values) that guide their mission. Holding true to such values as *respect, fairness,* and *integrity*, for instance when planning an activity, service, or product means that the group remains focused on core values while deciding what is important regarding future initiatives. Too many families and organizations get blindsided by exciting opportunities or by unforeseen hurdles and begin to violate the values that they have thus far held close.

   A comparable kind of thing happens when groups decide to go in a different direction because of similar scenarios that are not aligned with the overall purpose of the group. This kind of mindset can divide groups into factions, creating turmoil and conflict. Diversifying from an original mission can however turn out to be a positive thing if the team members are brought into the process where diversification is discussed and decided on.

4. *Determine the Objectives of Planning Early On.* Each activity, service, or product should have clear, understandable outcomes or objectives that are agreed upon by group members and that are clearly communicated throughout the

organization. Having understandable and realistic objectives provides a focus, a motivation, and a means to look back to determine how successful the planning process was. Depending on the group and the purpose of the planning, this can be fairly informal or highly structured. Because situations sometimes change and some variables are unforeseen, it may also be important to allow for some flexibility in meeting the identified objectives.

5. *Identify the Kinds of Resources Needed.* Conducting or developing any activity, service, or product will require a certain amount of resources so it is important to inventory what you have and determine what you will need. Each initiative will vary of course but resource categories often include the following (Weis and Gantt 2009):

   - *Space availability*—Evaluate the kind of space that may be needed for your initiative. Existing space is often the best and least expensive alternative but other space(s) may be necessary depending on the circumstances.
   - *Personnel*—In some cases family and organizational members are all that is needed for future activities, projects, or products but sometimes consultants and experts from outside the organization must also be considered.
   - *Finances*—Some initiatives require little operating money while others require a great deal. Conduct exhaustive research to determine how your group can get the most success from the least amount of money and to determine the best source(s) of financial support.
   - *Supplies*—Determining the kinds and quantities of supplies necessary is integral to being successful in every planning process.
   - *Equipment*—Another important consideration for success is the kind of and number of specific equipment necessary to make your plans a reality.

6. *Make Risk Management Priority #1.* Every activity, service, or product will inevitably involve risk; businesses have product recalls because of production errors and each of us encounters hazards every day at home, in the community, or on the highway. The purpose of risk management is to do everything possible to keep risk at the lowest possible level. A *risk* is considered anything that might impede the purpose of a group and include potential and real threats to individuals, income, property, or reputation (Weis and Gantt 2009).

   A classic list of strategies for handling risks was developed by Van der Smissen in 1990 and still provides value today. Van der Smissen suggests three components to managing risks:

- *Identification of Risk*—Before anything can be done regarding risks they have to be identified. Since there are obvious and less obvious risks a careful and thorough assessment in the identification component of risk management is important. For instance, family members vacationing in a mountainous area should know to stay together during hikes and have the proper equipment, supplies, and plans for different circumstances. Planning is important because certain parts of the terrain they are hiking in, coupled with sudden, unforeseen weather conditions can result in some perilous situations.

- *Evaluation of Risk*—Once risks have been effectively identified, they need to be evaluated as to potential occurrence and how severe the level of consequence might be should an accident, injury, or illness actually happen.

- *Handling Risk*—Van der Smissen proposes three basic ways to handle risk:

  ✓ *Prevention (Avoidance)*—Being sure that individuals have adequate training and knowledge regarding an activity, service, or product is an important way to prevent bad experiences.

  ✓ *Risk Reduction*—Clearly communicating safety rules and policies with individuals and maintaining good procedures of risk reduction will go a long way to keep risk to a minimum. Rules and policies need to be continually monitored by leaders.

  ✓ *Risk Retention or Transfer*—Once a family or an organization has decided to continue with an activity, service, or product it is important to have a plan for a loss, should one occur, or to transfer some of the loss to another institution, such as an insurance company.

Experts at nonprofit risk management centers propose four somewhat different strategies for managing risks (Ostrower and Stone 2006; Herman, Head, Jackson, and Fogarty 2004):

- *Avoidance*—Families and organizations may choose not to develop some activities, services, or products because they are deemed from the outset to be too risky. Despite the high risks involved, some activities, services, or products may seem too important to relinquish altogether and that is when another strategy, modification, can be considered.

- *Modification*—This indicates that something is so important that it should be implemented, but limits are required to reduce risks associated with various aspects of the situation. For instance, a swimming pool can be great fun for a family but the installation could be delayed until all of the family members reach a certain age; are fully able to swim; and can be used only while under strong adult supervision. A nonprofit organization that transports members from place to place may consider putting limits on the transportation system that might include the following (Weis and Gantt 2009):

✓ Double-check the validity of drivers' licenses as well as the safety record of drivers.
✓ Require all drivers to go to driver training and to pass a safe-driving test.
✓ Implement regular vehicular inspections, maintenance, and repair work.
✓ Maintain all documents that record each maintenance event or risk management procedure.

- *Retention*—Certain procedures or products may be deemed to be worth the inherent risks involved. In this case, families and organizations must be prepared to handle those risks should they become a reality. They need to look at the potential for risks and determine the consequences should those threats actually occur and identify the potential loss that would be associated with each situation. This assessment should be ongoing since situations change over time with the level of risks changing along with potential outcomes.

- *Sharing*—Transferring some of the risks involved with an activity or product to another organization or institution such as an insurance company is an important and common way to share the burden of various risks. Families and organizations should look carefully at the strengths and limitations of institutions that are willing to share some of these risks prior to formalizing their commitment. Keep in mind that completely transferring the burden or responsibility of a situation to another entity is impossible. For instance, a business may believe they have appropriate liability insurance for accidents, but the policy will not cover the damage to the organization's reputation should a preventable accident occur.

Risks are unavoidable and can never be completely managed away, but families, organizations, and businesses need to make risk management one of the highest priorities in all of their endeavors. Keeping risk to a minimum and developing ways to effectively manage risk can make all the difference in the world as to whether a family or an organization is successful or survives after disaster strikes.

7. *Communicate and Promote Projects.* As ideas and plans begin to take shape, it is important to share information and communicate both within the group as well as outside the organization in many cases. Families that plan vacation trips together need to share information on destinations, intentions,

and logistics to reduce unfortunate surprises as much as possible. Sharing this kind of information through family meetings can help to develop stronger relationships and happier experiences. Sharing some information with relatives, neighbors, and travel professionals can also be essential and even necessary in some circumstances. A comprehensive checklist of people to contact, tasks to address, things to pack, and individuals responsible for different aspects of the trip can be a lifesaver.

Promoting services and products for organizations and businesses is much more comprehensive and essential if they are to share the good news about their services and products. Most businesses have their own marketing department or hire consultants to present their products or services in the best possible way. Organizations form committees to develop public service announcements, flyers, websites, and other venues to create awareness about upcoming services or events that need to be shared with constituents. Marketing departments at colleges and universities can often be helpful in assisting nonprofit organizations and small businesses.

A ship in the harbor is usually safe; but that's not what ships are built for.

— African Proverb

---

8. *Develop a Project Budget.* Successful families and organizations often realize the importance of a budget. A *project budget* is nothing more than a projection of the *estimated expenses* that are associated with a particular endeavor and the *estimated income or revenue* that might be realized. The estimated expenses might include materials, supplies, rental space, travel, personnel, food, and telephone costs to mention a few. At times, families, organizations, or businesses have to generate additional money to cover the estimated cost of planned activities and sometimes existing funds are sufficient to cover the expenses. These groups might be able to pay for services and products from an existing budgeted income line or they might have to develop other ways of generating income, often through the project or service.

Keeping records of actual expenses and sources of income for each project provides great information to help determine if similar initiatives are warranted in the future. Even though some projects create deficit spending that has to be paid for through unrelated revenue generating activities, they might still be considered worth repeating for the benefits associated with the experience.

9. *Conduct a Project Walk-Through/Rehearsal.* Prior to conducting any activity or service, or developing any product, it is recommended to conduct a physical walk-through or rehearsal to examine as many aspects of the project as possible. If the scope of the event or project is significant, this sort of visualizing and assessing might need to be conducted numerous times. Visualizing what might happen and assessing all that is needed for a project can be a very valuable tool in keeping a project on the pathway toward success. A walk-through or rehearsal allows group members the opportunity to study procedures and assess most situations. Walk-throughs allow time to review the overall plan prior to implementation and suggest changes if necessary.

10. *Implement, Monitor, and Evaluate the Project.* Once the details are attended to, it is time to put plans into motion. Plans provide guidelines for how to proceed with a project, while the action step is when the ideas become reality. For any leader, returning to Part I of this book and reviewing some of the leadership concepts might be a good way to ensure that character and quality are incorporated into the leadership process. As soon as a project is off the ground, it is important to immediately begin monitoring the group's progress.

Monitoring and evaluating can be done informally or formally. For families, observation and discussion are often all that is needed to assess the effectiveness of an activity. Family leaders need to be sure to incorporate a process referred to as *active listening* and *understanding* in the monitoring process. During active listening an individual reflects back to a group member what the person perceives the speaker has said. This helps to clarify the communication process and ensure that everyone is on the same page regarding the progress of an activity.

**Setting a goal is not the main thing.
It is deciding how you will go about achieving it
and staying with that plan.**

— *Tom Landry*

Businesses and organizations might monitor the progress of a project in more formal ways; through interviews, focus groups, and surveys for instance and they can use the same process for evaluating a service or product once completed. Each activity, service, or product is a candidate for improvement, so monitoring and evaluating projects is critical to long-term success.

11. *Record Results and Formulate Recommendations for the Future.* Conducting good evaluation processes provides valuable information that can be useful in the future. Keeping records and documents about the successes of family activities and initiatives can provide family members with information. Documentation on trips, renovation projects, repair work, school reports, health matters, and many other areas is essential for family members to remain informed so they can make good decisions. Organizations and businesses often maintain records on their projects for the same reason; to stay informed of their successes and to see where changes might need to be made in the future.

Making recommendations on future initiatives based on past experiences allows groups an opportunity to explore possibilities from a more informed perspective. Recommendations for modifications often occur during a debriefing session held immediately following an event. According to Jennifer Newman and Darryl Grigg (2007), directors of *Newman and Grigg Psychological and Consulting Services*, using a debrief session to enhance performance is important for learning and improvement. Giving group members time to reflect on their success and ways to improve provides the opportunity to have a voice in how the organization operates. Taking responsibility for a project's success creates a sense of camaraderie and motivates everyone involved. Information from these sessions should be recorded so that it will be readily available to group members to assist in future planning endeavors.

Strong leaders understand the importance of planning in the success of any group. The steps discussed do not necessarily need to be in this exact sequence and not all of the steps need to be considered for every project.

REFLECTION AND APPLICATION
REFLECTION AND APPLICATION

Think about some upcoming projects or activities you have in mind.

Which of the steps discussed earlier would you like to include in your planning process?

_____

_____

_____

_____

_____

_____

_____

_____

_____

_____

Which of these do you believe are most important? Why?

_____

_____

_____

_____

_____

_____

_____

_____

_____

_____

_____

_____

Are there additional steps that you believe to be necessary for successful planning? What are they?

_____

_____

_____

_____

_____

_____

_____

_____

_____

_____

_____

Empower Others with Encouragement, Education, and Training

One of the most important and exciting things leaders can do is to *empower* members of their group to become more confident, competent, and self-reliant individuals. Sharing power or authority with others is a process of empowerment and, in effect, allows others to develop influence, which is a key component of the leadership process.

Empowered individuals feel as if they are supported and encouraged by their leaders and often perceive having some control or being free to operate independently at times. Empowered individuals often feel a strong sense of pride in the accomplishments of their group and develop a deep commitment to the group's purpose and are highly motivated toward reaching that purpose (Edginton, Hudson, and Ford 1999).

Before a leader can adequately empower others, s/he must be empowered and able to share critical aspects of their family and/or organizational and corporate life. They must be able and willing to encourage and support others to develop their own talents and skills. Strong leaders have the knowledge, confidence, and desire to enable others; that is they feel comfortable providing training and encouragement to help develop leadership potential in others. In a sense, the leader takes on the role of a coach who trusts individuals to work well within a clearly defined framework, avoids close supervision, and reflects with individuals on progress of various projects (Eisenberg and Goodall 2004). Empowered individuals are encouraged to have contrary views from the mainstream and to use their sense of confidence to transform the group they are involved with.

Empowerment includes the sharing of power or influence and decision making and usually occurs through a process of delegating and motivating individuals to higher levels of self-efficacy (Eisenberg and Goodall 2004). Although an empowered person feels a healthy sense of freedom that can result in a great deal of creativity, a clear sense of parameters and boundaries still needs to be understood by the individual and the leader. As a leader's faith in the character and abilities of an individual grows, the boundaries might also expand; or even contract under certain circumstances.

There is a danger in delegating too much too quickly or in delegating with too little supervision. Individuals who are delegated too much too quickly often feel overwhelmed and lack the confidence and competence to work on a project effectively. Too little supervision or lacking a monitoring system can result in dire consequences as well. There is also danger in delegating too little too late. Some individuals are ready, willing, and able to take the reins of a certain project, but their leader is unable or unwilling to allow that person the opportunity to take the initiative. This can result in a situation where the individual feels stifled and frustrated with the group.

The most effective delegation comes when leaders take the time to sit down with individuals and ask questions to develop a keen sense of where each person is regarding motivation and competencies. The leader can go on to make an informed decision about how much freedom and control an individual needs and be able to adjust when the situation calls for it (Hersey and Blanchard 1977).

Delegation with any activity or project, which can lead to feelings of empowerment, should only occur after individuals have been effectively educated and trained in the areas they are interested and involved. When both the leader and individual are aware of certain established or developing competencies, the delegation can occur. Because everything is changing at such a rapid pace, leaders need to maintain ongoing training so that individuals can continuously learn and develop. It is important to remember that individuals learn in different ways and rates. A good leader will make efforts to match opportunities with the needs of the individual (Eisenberg and Goodall 2004).

Education is not the filling of a pail but the lighting of a fire.

— William Butler Yates

As training occurs, a leader must maintain good communication with individuals to assess where s/he is in the learning process and how motivated each person is regarding the various tasks or projects. This provides the leader with the knowledge that helps to determine what level of trust and freedom an individual should have. Ongoing communication will help determine when the level of trust needs to be increased or pulled back. Another important piece to the empowerment package is to offer rewards to individuals when they have been trained and empowered, resulting in successful accomplishments.

Leaders in families and businesses cannot always provide the appropriate kind of education and training for each situation. Therefore, many families and organizations often rely on others for teaching, coaching, and consulting services. Professional trainers are sometimes in a better position to determine an individual's training needs and are better prepared to offer that training. It is critical that leaders carefully select those who are providing educational and skill development services.

A father or mother may not be able to teach their children how to be the best gymnasts possible but they can certainly guide them to a coach with great knowledge and character. They can support them in their efforts and empower them as talents grow. A school administrator might not have the capacity to provide faculty members with the knowledge and skills they need to teach with technological competencies but he/she can contract with a proven business in the field to be certain that faculty members are competent in that integral part of teaching and learning.

Before any plan of action is determined, it is best to sit down with the parties involved and identify the areas that need addressing with education and training. Brainstorming, self-analysis, reflection, and other discussion methods can help to determine what individuals need and want in the way of training and support. Discuss various alternatives for delivering the best education and training system(s) and choose the system that seems to work for the situation. Like other decisions, the alternative selected needs to be monitored and evaluated for value and possible modification or change.

As long as it is implemented well, empowering others within a group is one of the most important and exhilarating things that a leader can do. Empowered individuals are more competent and confident; they feel a stronger sense of freedom, independence, and creativity; and usually maintain a stronger commitment to the mission of the group. Working together, empowered individuals often achieve success beyond expectations.

REFLECTION AND APPLICATION

What are you currently doing to empower individuals in your work group or family?

_____

_____

_____

_____

_____

_____

_____

_____

_____

_____

_____

How successful do you think these processes are and why do you think that?

_____

_____

_____

_____

_____

_____

_____

_____

_____

_____

_____

What are additional ways in which you could empower others even more?

_____

_____

_____

_____

_____

_____

_____

_____

_____

_____

Budgeting and Stewardship of Resources

We all have limited resources, therefore budgeting and planning is vitally important for success. Estimating how much income or revenue will be needed to operate and how much money we plan to spend is critical in order to remain solvent. Before going through a step-by-step process for developing a budget, it is recommended to keep a few important tenets in mind while thinking about the budgeting process. Remember that family and organizational leaders do not necessarily have to be experts in each of the three competency areas. When expertise in an area such as budgeting is lacking, as long as they are willing to collaborate with those who have that expertise, success can achieved.

1. Prior to developing a budget, the leader needs to sit down with group members and discuss the *principles* and *purpose* that the organization has developed. This will make it easier to establish priorities for perusing projects and activities requiring financial resources. A leader that is concerned about the environment, for instance, should consider environmental variables in making financial decisions for a family or business to maintain a high level of congruity between the mission and the organization's activities.

   A family that is very interested in higher education for their children must concentrate on details regarding the cost of that experience. They must identify ways to cover educational expenses while maintaining a lifestyle that keeps everyone healthy and happy. A business leader with a vision for diversification and growth must consider ways to cover the cost of expansion while maintaining current operations.

**And the Lord God took the man,
and put him into the Garden of Eden
to dress it and to keep it.**

— Genesis 2:15
KJVB

---

2. Significant consideration should be given as to whom to *invite* to the budgeting planning process and input should generally be welcomed. Bolman and Deal (1994) note the importance of inclusion at every level of leadership. Leading others requires enlisting the emotions of others to share their vision. This sharing of ideas is the essence of inclusion.

Family members that are asked their opinions on financial matters will develop more self-efficacy, especially if their input is genuinely considered. Additionally, each individual contributes a different point of view, adding further information to the budget puzzle, creating a situation where relationships can flourish.

In organizations, as with families, it is equally important to hear from as many individuals as is realistically possible. Inclusion provides members with the feeling of importance and self-worth, helping to strengthen the feeling of teamwork and commitment to the organization. The additional information from a number of individuals can also make a huge difference on the bottom line.

Many families and organizations develop an *operating budget* for each year which can then be broken down into monthly or weekly plans. Organizations usually develop a budget for the *fiscal* or financial year, which can run concurrently with the calendar year. Organizations usually choose a period that is most beneficial for their operating cycles, such as July 1st–June 30th or September 1st–August 31st. Families, for the most part, operate on a fiscal budget that usually coincides with the calendar year.

Since budgeting is a form of financial planning or management, it is important to consider specific guidelines. Remember to keep the principles and vision of the group in mind when developing the budget and to invite as many individuals as is realistic to potentially help the budgeting process. The following guidelines for developing a budget were developed in part by Wolf (1999) and Weis and Gantt (2009).

Step 1: Develop a List of Possible Expenses. Budgets for most organizations are prepared months in advance of their implementation and it would be wise for families to follow the same timeline. Planning well ahead of an event allows time for researching the cost of items and services, and provides a period for individuals to share information.

While preparing a list of expenses it is useful to review previous expense lists for similar events to determine if the items are needed again or to determine whether costs have changed. It is also important to examine any new expenses that might be a part of the upcoming budget year. Expenses should always be projected on the high side in order to help account for any unexpected costs. Families and organizations must also strongly consider including a *contingency/reserve fund* or process to allow for unforeseen emergencies or to plan for special expenses that require a larger than normal outlay of funds, such as college tuition for families or capital outlays for corporations.

Step 2: Determine Potential Sources of Revenue or Income. After projecting expenses for the coming year it is necessary to determine how those costs are going to be funded. The best way to do this is to look at revenue/income from the previous year and determine if the level of finances is projected to change for the coming year. Depending on the expenses projected and any changes in estimated revenue/income, some families or organizations might wish to look at new sources of potential revenue. Income projections are best kept on the low side with flexibility for potential shortfalls.

After completing the entire budgetary process, if additional revenue or income needs to be acquired, round-table discussions with key group members, along with family financial planners or corporate financial specialists, committees, and/or consultants, can be instrumental in determining the best possible alternatives.

Step 3: Compare Expense and Income or Revenue Projections. Following a careful review of projected expenses and revenues, it is time to evaluate whether or not the projected revenue or income will be adequate to cover or exceed projected expenses. If the projected income/revenue adequately exceeds projected expenses, it might be time to invite those involved in the budgetary process to meet and discuss acceptance of the budget.

If careful review of revenues and expenses reveals a negative cash flow, there is a need to consider a different type of budgeting. One significant way to reduce expenses in the budget is through a process referred to as *zero-based budgeting.* Zero-based budgeting includes taking each line item in the budget to a theoretical zero level where no historical base provides justification for the expense. In this process each line item must be considered anew. For instance, telephone costs are something that both families and organizations must deal with. Instead of starting with the basic cost for telephone expenses from the previous year, we start with a theoretical zero base and work on ways to keep communication costs as low as possible for the coming year while maintaining quality.

For instance, changing carriers can bring a significant change in costs and negotiating for an even lower price with the company being considered might make it even better. Another alternative would be to encourage more e-mail communication and develop a policy that is fair but puts some limits on non-essential long distance calling. Making these three changes alone in the way telephone expenses are incurred can save families hundreds and organizations thousands of dollars.

Zero-based budgeting provides individuals with the opportunity to examine each expense line of a budget and to make some significant changes. The process is time-consuming and can be controversial, so it must be administered wisely. If the expenses of a budget are reduced to realistic figures and expenses still outweigh income/ revenue, then it is time to look for additional income/revenue opportunities.

Step 4: Setting Activity and Project Priorities. Once everything is done to reduce projected expenses and develop realistic income/revenue opportunities and a budget still does not balance, then it might be time to prioritize items and make some hard decisions. Group members will be required to ask each other the following questions.

1. Which activities or projects are central to the purpose and vision of the group?

2. Which activities or projects are costing more than they are worth?

3. Which activities or projects can be altered or eliminated without endangering the overall success of the group?

These are hard questions to ask, but perhaps necessary in order to develop priorities and to move on with financial soundness.

Step 5: Adjust and Balance the Budget. Once all of the expenses and income/ revenue have been carefully considered and priorities set, it is time to write the figures on a budget sheet with expenses in one column and income/revenue in a second column and be sure that the totals balance. Remember to place a reasonable and realistic figure in the contingency/reserve fund for unforeseen expenses and growth or new ventures.

Since the budget has been developed with projected expectations on the high side for expenses and on the low side for income/revenue it is conceivable that there might be money remaining and the budget is out of balance. If this occurs, the projected extra amount can be added to the contingency/reserve line for reasons mentioned above.

You cannot keep out of trouble by spending more than your income.

— Abraham

Step 6: Time for Budget Approval. Although families operate within different parameters than organizations and businesses, it is important for the leaders of a family to share the proposed budget and to understand the financial boundaries that the family is operating within. Sharing the completed draft of a proposed budget with other family members should be considered but might not be realistic, depending on variables such as age and confidential information. If members of a family are invited to review the draft of the budget, they should be encouraged to ask questions or make suggestions. Remember, a budget is merely a projection, while reality can be quite different. Therefore, once information is shared, members should be better prepared to handle discrepancies between projections and reality.

Organizations and businesses operate with a different mind-set of course, and the budgeting process will vary depending on policy and procedure guidelines such as by-laws, constitutions, or legal requirements as to how a budget is derived and approved. Generally, the budget is developed by key financial planners with the help of those in the trenches. It is common practice for first approval to be given by a budget committee, prior to going to a broader overseeing board for final approval. At each stage of the approval process, questions should be encouraged and suggestions invited and genuinely considered.

Step 7: Monitoring and Amending Effectively. Once a budget has been developed and accepted, it needs to be monitored carefully. Implementing and managing budgets successfully takes just as much attention as the planning phase, if not more.

Family leaders need to monitor the budget on a weekly and monthly basis to be sure that the expenses and income are happening according to plan. Key organizational staff members, under the supervision of an organization's board, are selected to carefully monitor organizational finances and to report to specified groups as to the operational success of a budget.

It is not uncommon for groups to amend budgets within a budgetary year as needed. Usually, this happens when there are unforeseen expenses, but it can also occur when income/revenue exceeds projections. However, if a budget has been carefully prepared, it might only need one or two revisions a year if any. Making no more than one or two revisions a year provides some flexibility without generating confusion.

Input is integral for revised budgets just as it is for an original budget. Family leaders can make these revisions easily and without a great deal of fanfare. Organizations, on the other hand, often have restrictions, guidelines, and policies as to the number of revisions that can be made, the types of revisions, and the process for the revisions including the policy regarding officially approving the budget.

Another important consideration in the budgetary process for both families and organizations is the concept of *cash-flow* which is projecting a family or an organizations income and expenses on a month-to-month basis as well as an annual basis.

During certain months or seasons, expenses might be higher or lower than usual just as income/revenue might fluctuate. Families and organizations must anticipate these potential circumstances and be prepared with income/revenue that is adequate to meet the expenses for each month. One way to do this is to have an adequate *contingency fund* that can be used for various situations. Another way to prepare for unexpected expenses is to maintain good relationships with lending institutions where a readily available line of credit can be made available and to be as aware as possible of low or no interest loans.

Stewardship is about accountability, which is essential in all leadership situations. According to Mark Miller, author of *The Heart of Leadership* (2013), to be the best possible steward, a leader needs to live with an understanding that the day will come when s/he will have to give an account for what was done with what was given.

Family and organizational leaders should also consider the concept of *stewardship* which implies managing one's own resources as well as maintaining a respectable regard for the rights and resources of others. Taking the role of stewardship seriously would mean that family and organizational leaders should not only consider their own group's well-being when making plans for using resources but also consider the well-being of others. This can sometimes seem like a daunting task because the world is competitive. Remember, good group leaders can be competitive and still respect the well-being of other individuals and groups by maintaining integrity and fairness in all transactions.

A great way to help instill the concept of stewardship in group members is by sharing resources such as time, expertise, energy, and money with youth, human service, and other nonprofit organizations. This provides support to those organizations and instills pride and a sense of bonding among group members as well. This sense of stewardship needs to be shared with all group members. Individuals should be encouraged to continue what can become a distinguishing characteristic of the group.

**The one principle that surrounds
everything else is that of stewardship;
that we are the managers of everything
that God has given us.**

— Larry Burkett

REFLECTION AND APPLICATION
REFLECTION AND APPLICATION

A strong budget is almost always essential for the success of any work group or family.

Which of the budgeting steps mentioned in this section can help you in making your budget better (work group or family)?

_____

_____

_____

_____

_____

_____

_____

_____

_____

_____

_____

_____

_____

_____

_____

_____

_____

_____

_____

Are you already implementing the concept of *stewardship* with your group or family? If not, how can you initiate this concept in the future?

_____

_____

_____

_____

_____

_____

_____

_____

_____

_____

_____

_____

_____

_____

_____

_____

_____

_____

_____

_____

_____

_____

_____

_____

_____

_____

_____

Achieving a Balanced Life

Leaders in families and organizations often feel pulled in many different directions. It is important for each of us to do all that we can to maintain a *balanced life* so that we can reach our goals and help others reach their goals while keeping ourselves refreshed for all that we wish to do in life.

**On the tightrope of life, only one thing
allows us to move forward, and that one thing is balance.
Without balance we fall into chaos,
we fall behind, we miss out
on what true choices we have in life.**

— Laura Kangas

It is not uncommon for those in leadership roles to spend so much time concentrating on goals that they fail to take time to enjoy life and replenish their emotional reserves. It is amazing how much more productive and creative a person can be when relaxed than tired or anxious.

Maintaining a balanced approach to life allows leaders the opportunity to work toward the group's goals with a smile on their face and a skip in their walk. A balanced life is especially important for leaders in families and organizations because of the high expectations on their shoulders. Leaders also need to set a good example and help with guidelines for others to lead a balanced life. The seven keys below should help aspiring leaders and enable them to assist others attempting to stay focused on the group's purpose while engaging in other important aspects of life.

1. *Set and check priorities in light of your overall purpose in life.* The first key to maintaining a balanced life is to remain focused on the family or organization's mission and vision while realizing that all members of the group need to feel refreshed, reenergized, and need to experience and participate in many other facets of life. At the same time, group members need to hold tight to the principles and values that are part of the group's culture.

   The mission, vision, and guiding principles of the group are interconnected. While remaining focused on these three areas is critical, it is equally important that group members experience and participate in activities that refresh and inspire them to stay focused. Activities that might serve this purpose are presented below. It is the role of a leader to help group members stay focused on their collective purpose, to feel inspired and refreshed enough to continue their work.

2. *Keep stressors under control.* Stress is the physiological response of the body to conditions in the environment requiring adaptation (Nauert 2013; Selye 1976). Stress is often experienced when we perceive dangerous or uncomfortable circumstances, whether or not the perception is accurate. Lab research shows that some stress is healthy, particularly if it is short-term in nature (Nauert 2013). Stress in life is inevitable and a certain amount of pressure is important because it motivates us to reach our goals and meet certain needs. Although frequently viewed as a negative, there is evidence that some people seem to thrive in stressful situations.

   Stress activates the *sympathetic nervous system* which has an effect on the heart, muscles, and other parts of the body. Stress hormones flow to nearly all areas of the body resulting in an aroused state that assists with meeting the demands of the situation. Once the demands are met, stress levels typically subside and the body usually returns to a more calm state. Sometimes threats, perceived threats, or uncomfortable situations do not subside keeping the body in a constant state of alert. At times there are so many threats or perceived threats that the body never seems to recover from the alert. This continued state of high alert can lead to high blood pressure, heart disease, depression, anxiety, headaches, and other diseases associated with the immune system. Stress can also tear at the very fiber that holds a family unit together. In organizations, it can result in low productivity and morale, absenteeism, substance abuse, high turnovers, and an increase in accidents (Ivancevich and Matteson 1980).

   Stress can come from all directions; changes in someone's personal life, good or bad, can set off the stress response. For instance, even though getting married is generally considered a happy time, it is also a stressful time due to the inevitable changes in lifestyle following the ceremony. Other stressful events in personal life include divorce, separation, childbirth, death of a close relative or friend, or a move to another part of the country, to mention a few. Stress is also experienced by organizational dynamics when working with a wide variety of people, feeling pressured to succeed, and feeling overwhelmed with the workload and unappreciated for our part in the overall operation of the organization. Recently, scientists have documented the stressful effects of technology in the workplace (Tarafdar, Tu, Ragu-Nathan, and Ragu-Nathan 2007) in addition to interpersonal stressors.

**The older I grow, the more clearly I perceive the dignity and beauty
of simplicity in thought, conduct and speech;
a desire to simplify all that is complicated and to treat everything
with the greatest naturalness and clarity.**

— Pope John XXIII

Leaders need to understand the various sources of stress for most people and how to handle personal stress effectively so they can help others. The following areas of stress management can lead to improved health and happiness. As a leader, there will be opportunities to share these processes for stress reduction with others.

- *Set priorities according to your values.* Stress is sometimes the result of spending too much time on issues that are of little value and not enough time on areas of greater value. Too often we follow routines in an effort to be successful that actually lead to a stressful life when we fail to slow down and understand what is really important. Therefore, it is recommended that all leaders take time to assess what really is important in life and to make time for those priorities. As a leader, let group members know that you value the mission of the group but also appreciate other concerns in life, including their priorities.
- *Develop support systems.* One of the most important areas of stress management is sharing your thoughts and feelings with individuals you feel comfortable with and trust. For families, friends and other family members should be considered first as confidants, but sometimes professionals can be most helpful in dealing with individual, marital, and family concerns. In organizations, formal and informal colleague support groups and peer counseling can be very helpful in stress reduction. As with family situations, there are times when professionals should also be considered.
- *Create a healthy environment.* Providing an environment where individuals feel important and where they have a satisfying level of control over their environment is critical in managing stress. People under stress, whether at home or at work, also need opportunities to release stress through social, cultural, and recreational activities. Organizing trips to museums, zoos, or theme parks; kayaking on the bay; or participating in softball leagues can pull us away from daily grinds and transport us to happier experiences.

It is not stress that kills us, it is our reaction to it.

— Hans Selye

Other ways to handle stress include exercise, healthy diets, hobbies, music, time management, yoga, massage, tai chi, meditation, prayer, and community service. A few of these methods for handling stress will be discussed later in this section of the book. Norman Vincent Peale once said that "(People) have become so tense and nervous that it's been years since I've seen anyone fall asleep in church . . . and that's a sad situation!"

3. *Cultivate and maintain healthy relationships.*

Developing and maintaining close relationships is essential for experiencing a healthy, balanced life. Some might say that it is one of the most important factors leading to a balanced life because of the extraordinary need most people have for connecting with others and avoiding loneliness.

The supreme happiness in life is the conviction that we are loved.

— Victor Hugo

Like all living forms people need stimulation and one of the best ways to be stimulated is through human contact. Humans engage in *intellectual stimulation* by discussing our ideas with others by going to school, church, museums, and other venues where social interaction can occur. We share our thoughts and listen to the ideas of others and develop our attitudes, knowledge, and belief system in the process. People also need *physical stimulation.* Holding and shaking hands, patting each other on the back, looking at and being seen by others are all important for our well-being. *Emotional stimulation* is also important for good health. Being able to express our feelings through smiles, laughter, and tears and to experience those same feelings from others can be the basis of bonding for friendships, work relationships, and families (De Vito 2001).

Healthy relationships are those that have been nurtured and that seem to thrive for long periods of time. There is a sense of well-being and stability in healthy relationships and a sense that the individuals involved add to the quality of life of one other. Good relationships do not develop by accident, they require effort and attention. The areas discussed below can be used as tools to create and sustain us through life's interactions with others (Relationship-Helps-And-Advice.com):

- *Mutual Respect*—Having a healthy respect for the thoughts and feelings of another person is important, even when some of those thoughts and feelings differ significantly from our own. Mutual respect also implies that the individuals are generally comfortable with each other's decision-making processes.
- *Trust*—Having confidence in other people and to be counted on by others is essential for the development of trust. Trust is something that is earned through word AND deed. We need to feel safe, physically and emotionally, before we can develop trust in one another.
- *Support*—Individuals in healthy relationships support and nurture each other throughout, particularly in times of difficulty and stress. Support can come in many forms including emotional, physical, informational, spiritual, and instrumental support. It is important to know that someone is there for you when you need them most. It is also important to know who to turn to when in need of different types of support (Salovey, Rothman, Detweiler, and Steward 2000).
- *Honesty*—Sharing the truth with another person is significant in developing healthy relationships. You have to be able to trust and believe that this person will not ridicule or hurt you as a result of this exposure. Being true to yourself and the other person is essential in developing strong, lasting bonds.
- *Fairness*—Understanding another person, compromising, and collaborating with him or her in all aspects will lead to a stronger relationship; one that is based on each person carrying an agreed-upon and accepted share of the load. Individuals in solid relationships have a good understanding of these often unspoken expectations and limitations. Good relationships have a win-win foundation where each person benefits and experiences a sense of fairness.
- *Separate Identities*—Too often in relationships we believe the other person should be just like us; sharing our beliefs and attitudes and behaving in a certain manner. Sometimes we believe this so fully that we behave differently while attempting to become more like someone else. This approach seldom works. In fact, expecting someone to change everything for us or trying to change our behavior for someone else can put a lot of stress on a relationship. Appreciating differences between yourself and others, instead of trying to force change, can be enriching for many relationships.

- *Good Communication*—Positive, meaningful interactions involve *active listening* and *understanding.* Active listening includes hearing what an individual has to say and restating it to see if you understood what they intended to say. This response provides the other person an opportunity to clarify her/his intended message. Once there is an understanding of an issue, you can more safely move on to another matter.
- *Commitment*—Having a strong belief in another person, a commitment to the relationship is one of the most important considerations in a relationship (Weis and Gantt 2004). Relationships with a commitment can endure long and difficult circumstances and remain strong.

Developing closeness with others is critical for healthy and successful relationships. In the book, *The Seven Levels of Intimacy: The Art of Loving and the Joy of Being Loved,* Matthew Kelly describes the four areas of our lives in which we need to develop closeness with others: emotional, intellectual, spiritual, and physical. This author goes on to expertly describe ways that we can develop this closeness (Kelly 2005). We highly recommend this exceptional book.

Eighty percent of life's satisfaction comes from meaningful relationships.

— Brian Tracy

Healthy relationships are vitally important and can be the difference between a successful group and one that is in constant turmoil. Understanding and practicing key aspects of healthy relationships will help family and organizational leaders to develop good relationships and become role models for group members, providing guidance for others to follow.

4. *Manage time in light of priorities, not in 24-hour increments.*

Too often we feel overwhelmed with our responsibilities and the limited time available to fulfill them. We are used to going through each day completing tasks and running around in a whirlwind then feeling that we really did not accomplish that much. Part of the problem is that we place too much emphasis on things that are not important and not enough emphasis on things that are worthwhile. In fact, we each have the same amount of time as anyone else; it becomes a matter of how we decide to spend our time and following through on these decisions.

One key to managing time effectively is to realize that we have choices in nearly every facet of our lives, including how we manage one of the most important resources we have, our time. There is a tendency to believe we are slaves to time, when the truth is we have chosen the way it is being spent. Time is one of our most valuable resources and we need to spend it wisely because it is limited; but it is our choice as to how we spend it. Following the three guidelines discussed below can provide insight and support for managing time according to your choices.

- *Prioritize your time according to what you value.* The most important step in managing time effectively is to realize that you need to manage time around what is really important to you and not around the clock. First, there is a need to determine what the most important aspects of your life are at home and at work, and to prioritize your time around these. Begin by looking inside and deciding what expectations you have of yourself, as well as what your family, friends, and community members expect from you. Talk with family members and friends about expectations and decide what is realistic and effective for everyone involved. Next, repeat this process at work. Review the expectations of yourself and others. Work to develop an understanding of the significance of these responsibilities. You may wish to brainstorm with colleagues and your supervisor(s) and discuss these hopes and expectancies. Having clear expectations is essential in all areas of life and is essential in helping us prioritize our time.

The key is not to prioritize what's on your schedule, but to schedule your priorities.

Stephen Covey

- *Organize your time around your values.* Divide your time up into broad *areas* and *categories* (Raffoni 2006). Two major areas might be *home* and *work*. Time at home could be divided up into *categories* such as family time, home improvement, community service, shopping, recreation, or relaxing. Time at work might be divided into supervision, production, meetings, communication, and personnel enrichment. Categories can be added or subtracted, depending on the family or the organization. After you have selected your categories in each area, determine the approximate percentage of time you are spending on each category. After careful consideration, estimate the approximate amount of time you would like to spend in each category. Study these time calculations for accuracy. Check your calculations with someone you trust and are close to at home and work making adjustments to your calculations. How you plan to spend your time should be influenced by what you value and have prioritized accordingly.

- *Manage your time and life around your values.* Recognizing what you value and organizing your life around those tenets is important. If you do not implement the resulting plan, it is practically all for naught.

Motivate yourself to keep track of your time by using a journal or log to compare your results with the plan. If your plan seems unrealistic, it might need to be modified, but be careful to adjust it in line with your priorities. The more disciplined you are at first, the better. New systems or processes often seem awkward at first use. Sometimes it is necessary to work through those awkward situations to eventually achieve the desired results.

Life isn't about finding yourself.
Life is about creating yourself.

— Author Unknown

---

5. *Participate in and encourage civic engagement.* Encouraging family and organizational members to become more actively involved in civic matters provides leaders with opportunities to make a difference in their own communities. This is true of ordinary day-to-day events as well as less common situations that compel us to take a stand. An example of how leaders can make a difference at home or work might be the issue of smoking. Countless studies have proven beyond a doubt that smoking and the breathing of second-hand smoke is extremely hazardous to one's health.

Some communities and some states have organized campaigns to ban smoking from public and private businesses and places. Banning smoking can be controversial and complicated. Many people still smoke in spite of the known dangers, often smoking around children in spite of the known perils of second-hand smoke to the health of these youngsters. Exposure to passive smoke can cause asthma, bronchitis, or pneumonia and is especially dangerous to children and pregnant women.

Encouraging those you live and work with to get involved in organizing effective campaigns to limit smoking to areas where smokers are the only ones affected can be a great way to address an important social and health issue while developing a bonding experience for those involved with the effort. Efforts carried out entirely at home and work or tying into existing grass roots efforts can help to further develop the foundation of successful families and organizations. (It is important to note that smoking is still generally legal and it is important to respect the rights of smokers who are smoking within legal parameters.)

Encouraging those at home and work who are eligible to vote in local and national elections is yet another way to offer individuals the opportunity to make a difference and to feel an important part of a team that cares about the way communities and issues are organized and addressed.

6. *Make a difference in the lives of others.* Making a difference in the life of someone else through involvement at school, in a community service organization, or through a place of worship is one of the greatest ways to realize happiness and develop a more balanced life! Mentoring a child through the Big Brothers Big Sisters program, coaching a team in a YMCA flag football league, or ministering to the elderly and disabled in a nursing home can make all the difference in someone's life as well as providing you with one of the greatest feelings imaginable.

     Make time to explore your community needs by contacting your local United Way agency, school systems, organization of churches, or Chamber of Commerce to find out what kind of needs exist in your community and determine where your knowledge and skills can be of service. Leaders who volunteer their time for community needs make a difference and also serve as role models for family and organizational members. An even stronger statement can be made by leaders who not only give of their time and talents, but also encourage those around them to make a difference with others as well.

     The most important reason to volunteer your time is to make a difference in at least one other person's life. Studies and reports indicate that those who do volunteer work also have higher self-image than those who do not, and on average live longer, healthier lives. So it is a win-win for all concerned.

Life's most urgent question is: What are you doing for others?

— Martin Luther King, Jr.

---

7. *Take care of yourself.* Too often leaders are so busy with organizing and producing results that they do not take time to take care of themselves. Boldly put, this is a selfish practice. If you do not take care of yourself, you will reach your limits sooner and more frequently deprive others of the value of your presence.

The concept of *wellness* means to take responsibility for your own health by learning ways to stay healthy, initiating health-promoting habits, excluding harmful ones, and responding to your body's warning signals by seeing a health care provider. Keeping your body strong and well-nourished helps you avoid injury or disease. Maintaining an alert mind and high spirits can also help to reduce stress, anxiety, and other health complications (Wellness in Your Life 2005). Taking care of yourself helps you to be a better leader at home and work. The following areas are health factors that you can control. It is recommended to check with a health care professional prior to initiating the following recommendations:

- *Nutrition*: Living well begins by eating well. Before adjusting your diet, you need to have an understanding of what healthy eating is and is not. You also need to understand that changes in eating habits do not work unless there is a change in mindset or a change in your lifestyle that fits in with this healthier diet.

  Some target areas for change might include getting less fat in your diet by choosing low- or non-fat dairy products and by eating more fish, poultry, vegetables, and fruits and less meats, butter, and animal fats. Another target area is reducing sugar intake by cutting back on sweets in cereals, sodas, and pastries and reducing sodium intake by choosing unsalted or lightly salted snacks, processed foods, and condiments.

  It is also important to include more fiber in your diet by choosing whole grain breads, cereals, fruits, and vegetables. If you think you need to lose or gain weight, check with a nutritionist, dietitian, or health care provider in your community. For a more complete understanding of healthy diets, contact the American Dietetic Association at 800-877-1600 or www.eatright.org or contact the Food and Nutrition Information Center (fnic.nal.usda.gov).

- *Exercise:* Regular physical activity and exercise helps to prevent heart disease, stroke, diabetes, obesity, and osteoporosis. Additionally, it helps to manage high blood pressure and cholesterol (Just Move! American Heart Association 2003). Individuals who exercise on a regular basis tend to feel and sleep better, and have less stress. Activities to consider include brisk walking, bicycling, jogging, swimming, rollerblading, or playing racquetball, basketball, and tennis. If you are not currently involved with exercising, start slow with five–ten-minute intervals until you can build up to thirty minutes a day on most days of the week. You might also add weight lifting to build muscle strength. Remember to stretch before and after your workouts.

Before you begin your health improvement plan, consider your health and physical capabilities along with your interests. You might wish to get the advice of fitness experts or prefer to include family and friends in your routines when possible to add variety. Be certain you have the best equipment possible, including shoes and clothing, and stay hydrated at all times. Starting and stopping will not help, you need to make a commitment and be as consistent with your new routines as possible. Remember, always check with a health care professional prior to initiating physical activity and exercise and monitor your progress regularly.

Movement is a medicine for creating change in a person's physical, emotional, and mental states.

— Carol Welch

- *Travel:* Traveling can be one of the best attitude enhancers and a way to learn about other areas, cultures, people, and yourself. Getting away from it all can provide breaks from the monotony of daily activities at home and work and provide a world of adventure and/or relaxation. Traveling is a way to reconnect with friends or family and provide lasting memories for all involved. It can be another way to keep yourself refreshed so you can be your best.

- *Spiritual:* Spirituality is about connectedness with self, others, nature, or a higher power (Doswell, Kouyate, and Taylor 2003). Spiritual individuals are often hopeful and enthusiastic. They are generally optimistic that things will work out for the best and usually have a plan and a willingness to work toward positive results for all involved. Spiritual individuals are filled with emotions and possess a belief system in which good is stronger than evil. They believe in focusing on the good in ourselves and others to help generate successful outcomes. Tying spirituality to a religion can provide strength and resolve. Spirituality is believed to positively impact a person's health status (DiSante 2003). Research shows that people with higher levels of purpose and meaning, or spirituality, tend to be healthier

(Holt, Clark, Kreuter, and Rubio 2003; Konig 2002). These studies indicate that people associated with identifying the purpose or meanings in their lives are generally happier and healthier. Helping others find and practice their spiritual selves is a role that good leaders should welcome and practice.

The foundations of a person are not in matter but in spirit.

— Ralph Waldo Emerson

- *Rest:* For healthy minds and hearts it is generally suggested that we each experience down time each and every day. It is recommended that we strive for seven or eight hours of sleep each night. Energy is restored during rest and sleep, allowing us to continue with valued activities. We all need to set aside times when we can take a break or get some sleep. These protected times can be used for participating in a leisurely activity that we enjoy, or simply sitting down or recreating with friends and family. Leisure time recreation takes many different forms, but the most important ones for rejuvenating the spirit are those you enjoy and feel invigorated when doing. Yoga, Tai-Chi, prayer, and meditative activities are all processes that can restore energy and rejuvenate our thought processes while helping our bodies recover from the stress response.

  Getting enough sleep can be helped by cutting down on caffeine, eating less, especially later in the evenings, and eliminating tobacco use. Since nicotine and caffeine are stimulants, they can contribute to insomnia and lead to frequently waking up once you are able to fall asleep. Individuals with a consistent exercise routine tend to sleep better as do those who keep sleeping areas cool, dark, and who incorporate a fan or white-noise source to block out noises.

- *Other Lifestyle Changes:* Taking good care of yourself sometimes means changing your lifestyle. Some things you can do to take better care of yourself include limiting alcohol consumption and cutting out drinking altogether. Overusing alcohol can result in heart and liver problems or damage to the brain. Try to avoid people and situations that encourage drinking to excess and never drive while intoxicated. Drinking alone or drinking frequently to escape the pressures of life can lead to alcohol dependency. If you are drinking alone or too often, you need to be aware of the potential consequences and see a health care professional to assist you.

Another change you can make to take better care of yourself is to stop smoking if you do and avoid areas where there is environmental tobacco smoke (ETS), commonly known as second-hand smoke. Smoking and environmental smoke can lead to heart, lung, and respiratory diseases. Smoking cessation is one of the hardest things to do because of the strong physiological and psychological addiction associated with this behavior. Despite being difficult to achieve, quitting is one of the most important things a smoker can do to improve his or her health. There are lots of successful ways a health care provider or local health department can help someone who is interested in giving up smoking.

Maintaining a balanced life can be a lot of work, but it provides the foundation for success in all realms of life. Keeping yourself refreshed and healthy will enable you to be a successful leader at home and work, and it will also set a good example for others to follow. Leaders need to be aware that a balanced life is essential for everyone and to integrate processes to reach a balanced life for all concerned. How balanced do you feel your life is at present? What changes do you need to make your life more balanced? Are you willing to make the required changes? How might you assist others to balance their lives?

**Each second you can be reborn.
Each second there can be
new beginning.
It is a choice.
It is your choice.**

— Clearwater

REFLECTION AND APPLICATION
REFLECTION AND APPLICATION

How balanced is your life, at present?

_____

_____

_____

_____

_____

_____

_____

_____

_____

_____

_____

What changes do you need to make for it to be more balanced?

_____

_____

_____

_____

_____

_____

_____

_____

_____

_____

_____

_____

_____

What are you willing to do to make those changes? What do you need to commit to achieve a more balanced life at work and at home?

_____

_____

_____

_____

_____

_____

_____

_____

_____

_____

_____

What about other group and family members? How balanced are their lives and how can you assist them?

_____

_____

_____

_____

_____

_____

_____

_____

_____

_____

_____

Understanding and Developing Human Relations Competencies

Once a vision is realized and a plan is developed it is time to effectively share that plan with others. Human relation skills are considered by many to be just as, if not more, important than any other competency area for leaders. A number of human relation competencies are important at home and work. Some of the most important of these include motivation, conflict management, teamwork, and valuing diversity.

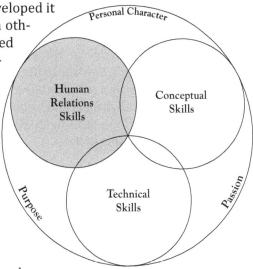

Creating a Motivational Environment

Motivation involves taking the initiative and providing the energy required to meet goals and to make a difference in the lives of yourself and others. People are motivated by their needs and the things they value. It is a leader's responsibility to help address the needs and values of others when working toward the goals of the family and/or organization. Before motivational processes can be implemented properly, a foundation of trust needs to be developed between the leader and members of the group. It is also essential for a leader to understand that individuals are motivated in different ways. A *motivational environment* can be created so that numerous and varied opportunities exist for individuals to be inspired and motivated.

Here are the building blocks deemed to be essential for establishing a foundation of trust that is required for a motivational environment to work:

1. *Integrity*: A leader of any organization must be someone that can be trusted and counted on for important matters. He or she must be perceived as someone who will be responsible for the well-being of all individuals and of the overall purpose of the group. Leading with integrity means standing up for the values of the group and maintaining those values and a high level of ethical standards even in turbulent times.

2. *Clear Goals and Purpose:* A good leader helps to develop clear and shared expectations for individuals in order to reach the goals and overall purpose of the group. Determining what the group is all about frequently involves developing a mission statement. This leads to sharing as individual and group goals are set. As group members work toward achieving these shared goals, bonding occurs, creating a sense of cohesion. Leaders need to articulate the process clearly and provide support for individuals and sub-groups in the process.

3. *Emphasis on Needs and Values:* Understanding individual needs and values and determining how those necessities and ideals fit in with the overall purpose of the group is essential in establishing a motivational environment. Individual and group values should be discussed and encouraged. We will take a closer look at individual needs and how they fit into the scheme of things later in this section.

4 *Concern:* One of the most important concepts that a leader in a business, organization, or a family should convey to others is that there is a *genuine* concern by the leader for group members. When group members believe that a leader has their best interests in mind, they are much more likely to develop a bond with that person and are more likely to trust the direction the organization is going.

**People don't care how much you know
until they know how much you care.**

John C. Maxwell

---

5. *Commitment:* Good leaders maintain a high level of commitment to the overall purpose of the organization or family and display behaviors that reveal that this common purpose is held in high esteem. Because of this high level of commitment leaders are more likely to keep group members focused on the activities and goals of the group.

Group leaders are not perfect individuals. Like anyone else, they make mistakes and occasionally stray from their values and goals. Whenever this happens, s/he must be able to admit these mistakes and make genuine and effective changes to regain the trust of others and to stay on track for the future.

> # I don't measure a man's success by how high he climbs but how high he bounces when he hits the bottom.
>
> — *General George S. Patton*

As the group leader establishes a foundation of trust with group members, a *motivational environment* is more likely to emerge. Although there are numerous motivational concepts that can be used in inspiring others, we are going to look at two that are held in high regard by many in the leadership/motivational field. In his book, *Developing the Leader Within You*, John Maxwell (1993) identifies five different factors that contribute to people feeling motivated:

- *Significant contributions.* Individuals are much more likely to be inspired if they feel like their efforts are appreciated and are making a positive difference. People need to feel as if what they are doing will have a lasting impact and that it is an effort that is contributing to achieving the group's goals.
- *Goal participation.* Involving others in determining the goals and mission of an organization allows them the opportunity to feel as if they have contributed to the development of the goals, which can lead to a higher level of ownership. Working together also creates the opportunity for considering a greater diversity of ideas and opinions during the goal setting process.
- *Positive dissatisfaction.* Dissatisfaction in almost any part of life can lead to a desire for change. Dissatisfied people are much more likely to have the energy and the motivation to drive change. With positive guidance, dissatisfaction can be used to generate new ideas and provide direction for change.
- *Recognition.* People generally feel motivated through personal accomplishments, but most individuals also like to be appreciated for the work they do. Often, appreciation can be expressed through a personal thank you and congratulations, while sometimes it needs to be expressed more formally.
- *Clear expectations.* Understanding what is expected of you is extremely important in relationships at home and work. It is essential to discuss tasks and develop guidelines to achieve the identified assignments. Enabling individuals to work toward their assigned tasks with effective monitoring allows them some control over their contributions.

When leaders establish processes that allow individuals to work together while developing goals, understand what is expected of them, and are encouraged for their efforts, an energetic *motivational environment* emerges.

**When we are motivated by goals
that have deep meaning,
by dreams that need completion,
by pure love that needs expressing,
then we truly live life.**

— *Greg Anderson*

Another motivational concept was developed by Abraham Maslow (1943) that still serves as a foundation for understanding human needs today. Maslow's concept is referred to as the Hierarchy of Needs Theory, in which he identified five basic areas of need: physiological, safety, affiliation, esteem, and the need to become self-actualized:

- *Physiological Needs.* Humans most basic needs are for food, water, sleep, and sensory gratification. Effective leaders recognize the significance of these needs and do everything possible to create a supportive environment so that those who have been entrusted to them can have these needs satisfied. Family members need to feel that their parents/leaders are doing everything possible to make them comfortable in this area. Employees must believe that their leaders are doing everything feasible to offer fair and meaningful compensation for their work efforts.
- *Safety and Protection.* Another important basic need for individuals is to feel that their home and work environment is relatively free from danger. It is imperative that leaders constantly evaluate the home and work environment to ensure that it is as safe as possible. Maintaining a safe home, in a safe neighborhood, allows family members to feel protected so they are able to focus on meeting other challenges in life. The same is true for employees and the presence of a safe work environment. Knowing that safety is acknowledged as being of the utmost importance is comforting and encourages individuals to move forward in addressing other areas.
- *Affiliation.* Another need that we all have is the desire to join or connect with others. Whether in the development of a family, or working with others to complete a task at work, the camaraderie and sense of belonging is satisfying.

When we feel cared for by someone or demonstrate that we care for another person, this need for affiliation is addressed. Leaders of families must help family members feel cared for and loved, while organizational leaders must ensure that employees feel that they are a significant part of the team.

- *Self-Esteem.* Individuals and groups typically feel better about themselves when there is a sense of achievement. This idea has been captured by the idea that self-esteem is earned, not learned. Another way of stating this is that people acquire a sense of significance, or positive self-esteem, from doing significant things, by being active participants in their own lives (Owens, Stryker, and Goodman 2001). This process can take the form of internal satisfaction associated with noting a sense of accomplishment, success, and knowing that they can be counted on. Or, the process can take the form of external satisfaction as when visible rewards such as a pat on the back, a thank you, or an allowance or salary increase is provided (Weis & Gantt 2009).
- *Self-Actualization.* Maslow believed that most people strive to become everything they are capable of becoming. Once they have reached a very high level in each of the basic areas, they develop the desire to reach out to others to assist them in reaching their goals and dreams as well. Leaders in families and organizations have the opportunity to encourage those who have reached high standards in various areas to assist others in reaching toward their goals and dreams.

Throughout his writings, Maslow indicated that it was important for individuals to meet their basic needs such as food, water, and shelter before attempting to satisfy higher level, more abstract needs, such as affiliation or self-actualization. An organizational leader who understands Maslow's concept, and is able to apply these tenets to real-world situations, can create a *motivational environment* that allows individuals to meet needs at various levels. A family leader can provide opportunities for individuals to share in meeting basic needs and to feel as if they are valued contributors to the well-being of the family; thereby contributing to the development of positive self-esteem.

Meeting our needs and goals, while doing what we believe is important, is fulfilling and motivational. Good leaders understand the complexities of inspiring others and strive to create the most effective *motivational environment* possible for others to share in. *Motivational environments* are supportive and offer a myriad of ways to help those involved find and reach their purpose in life.

REFLECTION AND APPLICATION

Each of us is motivated in different ways.

What are some of the areas you can change to "create" a more motivational environment for yourself?

_____

_____

_____

_____

_____

_____

_____

_____

_____

_____

_____

_____

_____

_____

_____

_____

_____

_____

_____

_____

_____

_____

What about creating a "motivational environment" for those in your family/organization? What would it "look" like?

_____

_____

_____

_____

_____

_____

_____

_____

_____

_____

_____

_____

_____

_____

_____

_____

_____

_____

_____

_____

_____

_____

_____

_____

_____

_____

_____

_____

Managing Conflict

Conflict is a normal part of life and can lead to positive outcomes when handled effectively. Discord often occurs when two or more parties disagree with each other regarding interests, ideas, goals, behavior, beliefs, or the use of resources and express that disagreement in some way.

Gone unchecked, conflict can lead to negative thoughts, feelings, or actions. Individuals involved in a disagreement sometimes feel defensive of their position and remain guarded toward the other individual(s) involved in the disagreement. This defensiveness in a family or organization tends to deplete energy and divert time and resources away from other important areas of interest to the group.

Managing conflict is far from easy, but essential for families and organizations to work together successfully. There are a number of *unproductive conflict strategies* that need to be avoided. For instance, *avoidance* both physically and/or mentally can leave a situation unresolved, leading to depletion of energy and effectiveness. *Non-negotiation* is an unproductive strategy where one of the parties refuses to discuss a conflict or *steamrolling* where one of the parties refuses to even listen to the other side and continues hammering their own points of view until the opposition gives in or leaves the group (De Vito 2001). There are lots of other demeaning, unproductive, unsuccessful ways to handle conflict that need to be carefully avoided.

On the positive side, when a conflict arises it provides individuals with the opportunity to face the problem head-on and to work together toward managing or resolving it. One model of conflict resolution that is effective involves the following steps (DeVito 2001):

- *Define the issue.* One of the most important steps in managing conflict is defining what the issue is actually about. Many times conflict can arise simply because the parties involved have a misunderstanding of expectations or actions. Therefore, it is important for all parties to be very specific with any and all concerns. Asking questions and confirming the other person's interpretation of the issue, while clearly stating your own, is a significant step toward resolving concerns.
- *Examine possible solutions.* The most successful solution is one that leads to a satisfactory solution for all parties concerned. In other words, each party feels as if their concerns have been addressed. A one-sided solution could result in immediate or even long-term resentment and additional conflict. When weighing the best potential solutions, discuss the ups and downs of

each option and the potential consequences for everyone involved to arrive at an equitable arrangement for all.

True peace is not merely the absence of tension; it is the presence of justice.

— Martin Luther King, Jr.

- *Test the solution.* Once a solution has been selected, test it out mentally to see how it feels from each point of view, for now and the future. Examine as many possible consequences as you are able to imagine. Each party should be involved in this exercise. Next, implement your solution and if it does not feel right to those involved, move on to the next option.
- *Evaluate the solution.* Once you have selected an option and tried it out in practice, you will need to get together and discuss whether the solution actually helped in resolving the conflict. Monitoring the progress of a solution is critical and needs to involve all parties. Ask yourself whether the positives outweigh the negatives.
- *Accept or reject the solution.* If the solution feels right to all parties, it becomes a more permanent part of the day-to-day operations. If there are still concerns, you can modify the solution or go back to the original conflict, examine it more closely to see if yet another resolution should be tried, and begin again.

There is another great model for conflict management that involves choosing from five options when faced with a conflict: *avoiding, accommodating, competing, compromising,* or *collaborating* (Borisoff and Victor 1998). While each of the options has its place, choosing one of the first four options may leave some portion of the conflict unresolved.

- *Avoiding.* Avoidance can actually be a very strong style of managing conflict if there is some risk of harm involved, otherwise conflicts have a tendency to grow if not addressed. Avoidance rarely results in conflict resolution and generally leaves all parties unsatisfied. A residual effect can occur if the conflict is never adequately managed, relationships can be damaged, and goals not reached.

- *Accommodating.* If one of the parties involved in a conflict is insistent that a certain path be taken while addressing an issue and that avenue is not unacceptable to other parties involved, accommodating an individual by giving in can be effective. However, once an individual or group accommodates another, they can sometimes be perceived as being easily taken advantage of, so accommodation should be considered carefully.
- *Competing.* When information provided to the group indicates one option is clearly beneficial over another, that option might need to be strongly promoted to become the group's choice. However, when there is not a clear-cut solution for an issue, this option can lead to disillusionment and dissatisfaction on the part of group members, thus leading to a divided organization and a negative environment. This option tends to discourage open and honest communication and generates unnecessary rivalries.
- *Compromising.* When there is not a strong, clear-cut direction for a group to choose, sometimes it may be acceptable to allow all parties involved to give some ground in order to reach a decision on a way to approach an issue. The downside of this style is that all individuals involved may feel somewhat disappointed for giving in and not satisfied that the sacrifices were equally made.
- *Collaborating.* When a group reaches a solution that makes sense to all involved, satisfaction and morale are enhanced. The collaborating approach to addressing an issue or conflict focuses on the best way to manage the issue rather than individual positions. This process generally takes a good deal more time and energy but more often results in a direction that can be embraced by group members. Collaborative solutions empower more people, who will be more likely to enthusiastically participate in conflict management in the future. The collaborating style of conflict management is the most desirable style for the majority of situations.

Effective leaders help group members learn positive ways to manage conflict and practice those methods for the good of the organization. In addition to the collaborative process described above, it is a good idea to approach conflict management with a *win-win* mindset as explained below:

- *Look at the conflict from the other person's point of view.* Understanding the other person's point of view provides you with more information and helps the other person see that you are attempting to be fair.
- *Use "active-listening" to hear and understand the other person's viewpoints.* Carefully consider what the other person is saying and ask pertinent questions.

- *Consider assistance from principled negotiators.* Sometimes the conflict may seem so monumental that solutions should be sought from individuals external to the conflict, which are valued and trusted by all parties involved.

Managing conflict is far from easy, but once a group has the information and guidance they need to address issues positively, it is a matter of practicing successful processes time and again until it becomes a part of the group's culture.

The most important single ingredient in the formula of success is knowing how to get along with people.

— Theodore Roosevelt

REFLECTION AND APPLICATION
REFLECTION AND APPLICATION

Think about a recent conflict that occurred in your family or organization.

How was it managed?

_____

_____

_____

_____

_____

_____

_____

_____

_____

_____

What ideas/concepts listed in this section could have been helpful?

_____

_____

_____

_____

_____

_____

_____

_____

_____

_____

_____

_____

Which of the ideas/concepts discussed in this section do you plan to use in the future?

_____

_____

_____

_____

_____

_____

_____

_____

_____

Building Great Teams

Encouraging others to work together can be challenging, especially in a culture that emphasizes competition and being the best. For families and organizations to work toward their common goals they must be supportive and understanding of one another and realize that it is much more effective to plan and reach goals cooperatively than competitively.

There are plenty of examples in business, sports, and families of great teams, but you only have to look out the window to find a great example of teamwork. Nature observers discovered some time ago that geese work exceptionally well together in flying south in the fall and back north in the spring (Weis and Gantt 2009):

- By flapping its wings, each bird provides uplift for the bird following and, by flying in the V formation, the reduction in drag reduces the energy cost of flying. This helps to almost double the distance that a single bird can fly.
- Soon after a bird drops out of formation it realizes the significant increase in drag and resistance to flying alone and quickly rejoins the flock.
- When the lead goose become tired or confused it drops back into the formation and another goose takes the lead.
- Birds in the back of the formation honk encouragement to geese in front to maintain their position and speed.
- Geese have strong bonds and when one goose becomes sick or hurt, two geese drop back and stay with the goose until it gets better or dies. These two geese fly together to join another formation or until they reach the original group.

People can learn a lot from observing geese; working as a team increases productivity and discourages nonproductive activities. Good teamwork provides an opportunity for individuals to take turns leading and feeling significant and empowered, and provides support and protection for team members when they are discouraged, weak, or make a mistake.

No one can defeat us unless we defeat ourselves.

— Dwight D. Eisenhower

Recent teamwork literature suggests there is no "I" in team but this does not mean that individual effort is not needed or appreciated. On the contrary, personal effort is critical to the success of a team. Successful teams encourage individuals to be the best they can be while contributing to the overall mission of the organization and contributing in a collaborative manner so that all benefit.

There are a number of successful concepts that have to do with developing excellent teams. Zoglio (1993) identified seven keys for a successful team: *commitment, contribution, communication, cooperation, conflict management, change management,* and *connections.* We will examine each of these briefly:

- *Commitment.* Understanding the overall purpose of a group and committing to that purpose creates bonding experiences that help to ensure that the group stays focused and works collaboratively toward success. To ensure this commitment, each member of a group must have an opportunity to take part in the development of the overall purpose and identification of shared values. Each member must have opportunities to contribute to developing the goals of the group and to feel recognized for their accomplishments.

**Teamwork is the ability to work together
toward a common vision.
The ability to direct individual accomplishments
toward organizational objectives.
It is the fuel that allows common people
to attain uncommon results.**

— Andrew Carnegie

Family leaders should hold discussions from time to time to review the overall purpose and goals of their unit such as love, support, encouragement, making a difference in the lives of others, religion, education, sports, and many other areas that families agree to focus on. Each family member should have an opportunity to make contributions to the purpose and should be recognized for their effort. Organizational members must also have an opportunity to contribute to the mission and they should feel accepted and be appropriately recognized for their involvement.

- *Contribution.* Each individual in a group must contribute something to the family or organization, recognizing that each person will make different contributions at various levels. Family and organizational leaders need to be encouraging, supportive, and empowering in the development of different attributes that individual team members bring to the group. New and advanced skills and mutually beneficial attributes should be encouraged through a supportive environment. Team members are much more productive when they feel they are part of the team, gain confidence in their contributions, and feel empowered.

Families and organizations can help group members to gain confidence by asking for individual input. Confidence will grow as these ideas are included in team activities and as individuals are recognized for their part in helping the group succeed. Effective and appropriate education and training, having required resources, support, inclusion, and recognition leads to empowered and contributing team members.

- *Communication.* One of the most important criteria for successful teams is that they are encouraged to communicate often, openly, and effectively. The team environment must feel safe and encouraging for individuals to ask questions and make suggestions without the fear of being judged negatively. Members must be able to make errors in communication without fearing reprisals or ridicule and be forgiven for mistakes when requested. Open dialogue often leads to exciting and productive ideas and an enthusiastic team culture.

  Communication can be more effective when team leaders encourage listening actively, are sensitive in their language use, offer and receive feedback with consideration for other people, trust and respect other people's positions, and are as efficient with meeting times as possible. Interpersonal skills can be developed through educational training, seminars, workshops, working with counselors, or participating in online webinars. Each of these methods should be considered when appropriate.

Never doubt that a small group of thoughtful, committed citizens can change the world; indeed, it is the only thing that ever has.

— Margaret Mead

- *Cooperation.* Working well together is critical to the overall success of a team. The world can be very complicated. Therefore, individuals need to share their information, concerns, and ideas in a selfless manner for the overall good of the group, which requires them to become *interdependent* (Covey

1989). We are all truly interconnected and working alone is usually not as productive. Cooperation helps to build synergy which leads to productivity, growth, and successful teams.

Smart leaders know how to encourage group members by serving as a role model for cooperation and by recognizing members for their cooperative efforts. They help ensure cooperation by demonstrating accurate and timely work, sharing progress notes with others, creating new ways to be successful and by encouraging a healthy, open, trusting home or organizational atmosphere.

Great discoveries and achievements invariably involve the cooperation of many minds.

— Alexander Graham Bell

- *Conflict Management.* Having a difference of opinion from someone else on different topics such as resource utilization, behavior, political beliefs, religion, and a number of other areas is natural. It is inevitable for disagreements to emerge, creating disputes. Conflict that is managed effectively can stimulate creativity and lead to more successful teams. When not managed well, issues can become more intense and future issues might not be addressed at all, which can lead to deception and complicated dynamics that adds to existing tension between individuals.

  Using effective models to manage conflict allows leaders in families and other groups to offer opportunities for individuals to work together to solve their differences. Successful conflict management often leads to positive, shared solutions which makes any group more effective. It also helps to develop trust and a stronger sense of camaraderie.

- *Change Management.* Change, like conflict, is inevitable. Families and organizations must be sensitive to potential changes that lie ahead and evaluate the variations that are coming so they can decide which areas of their group processes, if any, need to adapt to be successful. Some things such as group values or trusting relationships might never need to change. But other areas might require continuous modifications. Examples of items needing regular modifications include advanced instruments of technology and electronic forms of communication. Policies and procedures associated with these types of processes that assist the group in operating successfully will need to be reviewed regularly.

Family and other group leaders must be aware of upcoming change and be able to guide group processes so that members can work together in deciding what, if any, adjustments are needed to remain relevant and current. This requires a constant evaluation process where team members determine if group change is necessary to adapt to new circumstances or are necessary to achieve a higher level of success.

You must be the change you wish to see in the world.

— Mahatma Gandhi

- *Connections.* Small sub-groups invariably form in any family or organization for various reasons. Moms and dads form parental teams to discuss a child's development or ways to improve family communication. Organizational teams are formed to develop and promote specific products or to discuss ways to make the organization more financially solvent. Forming teams within a group is natural and often necessary. At the same time, it is important for leaders to monitor the progress of teams to make sure they: (1) connect with the overall purpose of the group, and (2) communicate with individuals these groups are attempting to serve.

  It is important that teams within an organization work in alignment with the mission and that their work serves their constituents. In a business, the constituents could be customers, clients, or patients. For families it might be other family members such as grandparents, aunts, uncles, and cousins or even individuals in the community. Making sure that teams serve constituents well and within the framework of the group's purpose is an important task for the leader. Recognizing group members who assist in completing those tasks assigned to a sub-group is important to achieving success.

  Another great concept for effective team building was developed by Susan Heathfield and published in *Your Guide to Human Resources* (http://humanresources.about.com/od/involvementteams/a/team_culture.htm). Heathfield states that it is important to foster a culture that is receptive for teamwork; one that encourages collaboration and where individuals share planning, decision making, and actions with each other. She further explains that a culture such as the one described can be created through the following actions:

- *Leaders communicate clearly that teamwork is expected.* Each person in a group must understand they are an integral part of a team and that they must work cooperatively to achieve success.

- *Leaders model teamwork through their work with others.* Unfortunately, for some leaders it is "do as I say, not as I do." Great leaders emulate the actions and values they expound.

- *Teamwork must be on record as being a significant part of the culture.* When values are discussed and itemized within the group, teamwork should always be an integral part of the list.

- *Leaders reward and recognize responsible team members.* Team members who demonstrate collaboration receive higher recognition and rewards than those who try to work in isolation.

- *Leaders provide consistent and effective communication relevant to teamwork.* Good leaders consistently provide information to team members regarding their collaborative efforts. This feedback helps individuals focus on the significance of teamwork.

  Individuals working together effectively can accomplish so much more than people working separately. Not only are individuals more successful working as a team, but they also bond during teamwork activities and develop a more important feeling of belonging. It is a key responsibility of leaders in families and organizations to work tirelessly to bring individuals together to form strong partnerships and teams. How would you rate the team-like qualities of the groups that you lead? Reflect on the concepts provided and imagine how they might help your group become an even stronger team. Make a concerted effort to incorporate these ideas within your group.

Coming together is a beginning, staying together is progress, working together is success.

— Henry Ford

REFLECTION AND APPLICATION

On a scale of 1 to 10 with 10 being the best, how would you rate the team-like qualities of the groups you are a leader of or involved with? What can you do to improve as a "team" leader?

_____

_____

_____

_____

_____

_____

_____

_____

_____

_____

Which of the concepts listed in the previous section could help your work group or family become an even stronger team?

_____

_____

_____

_____

_____

_____

_____

_____

_____

_____

What concerted effort will you make to incorporate these ideas within your work group or family?

_____

_____

_____

_____

_____

_____

_____

_____

_____

_____

_____

_____

_____

_____

_____

_____

_____

Embracing Diversity

According to some projections, by the year 2030 Asians, Hispanics, blacks, and other minorities will make up about a third of this country's population. Senior citizens will also make up a larger portion of the workforce than ever before as the baby boomers, born between 1946–1964 enter their golden years. Additionally, thanks in large part to the Americans with Disabilities Act of 1990, disabled individuals are contributing to the workforce like never before. Our country's demographics are changing quickly and education and business organizations are responding by requiring individuals to acquire knowledge and skills in cultural competence (Allen 2004).

Business operations have shifted to encompass a more global economy. There are very diverse customers, clients, and suppliers in the marketplace (De Janasz, Dowd, and Schneider 2002) and businesses must be prepared for this shifting landscape. Educational institutions are constantly restructuring to accept and educate students from all corners of the world, and members of families must be well-prepared for diversity in their workplace and community.

Regardless of differences in age, gender, nationality, race, ethnicity, religion, abilities, and other factors, group members share a number of similarities. They each feel the need to belong and to know that their membership in the group is important. This is as true for a family unit as it is for all other groups. Our country and world is made up of individuals from all kinds of backgrounds so it is imperative that leaders help group members gain knowledge, understanding, and acceptance about various differences in others so they can share positive experiences and be more effective in various situations. In a multi-cultural world, becoming culturally competent is not only the practical approach but it is also the right thing to do.

> **Diversity is the one true thing
> we all have in common.
> Celebrate it every day.**
>
> — *Anonymous*

Cultural competence, what is it? Culture can be broadly defined as a distinctive pattern of beliefs and values that develop among a group of people who share the same social heritage and traditions. Culture is the whole way in which a group of people has learned to live. There are many dimensions of culture including language, political, economic, geographic, aesthetic, scientific, ecological, anthropological, sociological, psychological, philosophical, and theological (Thompson and Cuseo 2012). According to Kuh and Whitt (1988), culture refers to the deeply embedded patterns of values, beliefs, and assumptions that shape the way in which an institution or group behaves.

Competency refers to the ability to understand and respond effectively to human needs based on these cultural variations. Thus, diversity is a feature of the population, and competency is a measure of effectiveness (Thompson and Cuseo 2012). To achieve competency in dealing with our diverse society, we must develop an understanding that our internal biases have affected those around us, both those we know personally and those we do not know. This understanding would bring us to a state of cultural awareness. As we gain this awareness, we become more capable of acknowledging our differences, accepting these distinctions, and taking action accordingly.

The ultimate goal is achieving cultural competence. According to Thompson and Cuseo (2012), this involves the ability to appreciate cultural differences and to interact effectively with people from different cultural backgrounds.

Unfortunately, there are a number of hurdles to understanding and accepting others who seem different from what we are used to. Many individuals around the globe grow up believing their culture is the best, while all other cultures are inferior. This is referred to as being *ethnocentric.* It is a condition that significantly limits personal growth and effective interactions with others. Some believe that individuals who share a certain trait, such as skin, hair, or eye color are all alike; this is referred to as *stereotyping.* Stereotyping is inaccurate and unfair and it also limits interpersonal communications and teamwork. Those who stereotype often go to the next level and pre-judge individuals based on these stereotypes, a term referred to as being *prejudiced* or making decisions about someone before even meeting or interacting with them. Those who pre-judge others often *discriminate* toward those individuals meaning they act in a certain way based on their prejudice, which was based on the stereotype they made.

These unfortunate errors in thinking and judgment have led to countless misunderstandings, disagreements, and conflicts. Therefore, dispelling these beliefs or helping to put them in proper perspective is challenging but critical if groups are going to work well together and succeed. This is a challenge that family and organizational leaders have to address for the sake of all individuals involved in the group process.

**If we cannot end now our differences,
at least we can make the world safe for diversity.**

— *John F. Kennedy*

There are a number of positions a leader can take to help group members embrace diversity effectively:

- *Awareness.* First, a leader needs to become aware of his or her culture and how that culture shapes the way that life and people are perceived. It is important to recognize potential biases or stereotypes and to be able to deal with those preconceptions effectively and fairly. A bias is an evaluation or an attitude, which is difficult to change. Despite this, a leader must be open to positive change in order to share effective concepts for embracing diversity with other group members. Being aware of and respecting differences in others is also critical in the early stage of embracing diversity.

- *Provide Information on the Importance of Embracing Diversity.* A good leader should help others in the group become aware of their potential biases and recognize the importance of diversity for practical and ethical reasons. Leaders should go over some of the hurdles that exist on the way to effective cultural competency; overcoming stereotyping, prejudices, and discrimination for example. Becoming aware of one's own culture is critical to understanding the importance of valuing one's own culture as well as that of others. A dialogue of ethical and practical reasons for embracing diversity needs to become part of the fabric of the group's formal and informal processes. Discussions should include the importance of embracing diversity and striving to achieve cultural competence in working toward the mission of the family or organization.

- *Empower Others through Training, Experiential Activities, and the Group Environment.* Training for cultural competency can include classes, workshops, and experiential activities. Classroom and workshop activities can be initiated by connecting with local educational or religious institutions, checking with the local Chamber of Commerce, or by doing an online search for experts in cultural competency in your area. Classroom work needs to be followed up with activities in which individuals from different backgrounds work together to address simulated or real situations in a structured setting. Making the most of individual differences in solving problems helps to develop bonds and trust across different backgrounds. Along with these processes, family or organizational leaders must develop and promote a comfortable environment for all group members to share. This environment should include appropriate rewards for embracing diversity in working toward the group's mission.

- *Serve as a Role Model.* If a leader is to be successful in helping to create an effective, culturally diverse group, they must be perceived as a person who embraces diversity for its many benefits and as a person who discourages bias and unfairness. Achieving this will help tremendously in providing guidelines and encouragement for others and setting the stage for positive relationship building and greater successes overall.

Strength lies in differences,
not in similarities.

— Stephen Covey

- *Monitor Progress and Make Adjustments if Necessary.* Like any significant part of a family or organization, the development of a successful culturally diverse group and environment must be monitored and adjusted if and when necessary. Informal or formal interviews, surveys, focus group meetings, or observations can provide information on whether groups are headed in the right direction regarding cultural competency.

Embracing diversity is the right thing to do. People from different backgrounds can work together to complement their individual differences. This leads to creative and synergistic efforts toward the group's mission. "If a group is unified, it is capitalizing on its diversity with everyone adding his or her perspective—way of thinking and way of acting—to each and every challenge faced by the group" (Weis and Gantt 2009). Reflect on the importance of developing groups that embrace different cultures. What can you do to help your group become more culturally competent?

REFLECTION AND APPLICATION

Do you have a good understanding of how important it is to develop groups that embrace different cultures? Explain why diversity is important to you and your groups.

_____

_____

_____

_____

_____

_____

_____

_____

_____

_____

_____

_____

_____

_____

_____

_____

_____

_____

_____

_____

_____

_____

_____

_____

_____

_____

What can you do to help your group become more competent in interactions with individuals from diverse backgrounds?

_____

_____

_____

_____

_____

_____

_____

_____

_____

_____

_____

_____

_____

_____

_____

_____

_____

_____

_____

_____

_____

_____

_____

_____

_____

_____

EPILOGUE

Families, businesses, and other kinds of organizations deserve the very best leadership possible. If there was but one formula for effective leadership it would be documented in every textbook, book, journal, and magazine that dealt with the subject of leadership but there is not. No two concepts, leaders, or situations are exactly alike. Therefore, it is important that leaders of various groups understand the need to find their own path to becoming the best leader possible through exploration, study, and experience. Leadership is about making a difference in situations and lives. Good leaders are highly desired because it takes an enormous amount of talent and character to inspire and guide others consistently and effectively.

We reaffirm our belief that *good leaders are made and not born.* If you want to make a difference and lead others in the quest for success, you must be willing and able to study, understand, and initiate ideas and concepts that can enable you to become a better leader. The revised *Integrated Leadership and Character Model* has as its core leading with *character, purpose,* and *passion.* Using this model can result in leadership that is respected and trusted. Group members feel confident in leaders that have good character; they have a clearer and stronger focus when the purpose of the group is communicated effectively and consistently. They can develop a stronger commitment to the group's purpose when passion is shared and nurtured. It is also important for leaders to possess or develop conceptual, technical, and human relation skills or be able to collaborate with others who are competent in these areas since they are also critical to the success of most groups.

The revised *Integrated Leadership and Character Model* can be an excellent guide to help you assess and develop your own areas of strength. It can also assist in assessing and developing strengths in those around you. It has been presented to organizations nationally and internationally for use in the selection and training of staff members and has been found to be equally helpful in the development of group members in organizations and families. Incorporating the model into your leadership style may require a transformational commitment to change, which often requires dogged determination to make it happen. Others will also need to be receptive to this change. It might be difficult, but if it helps you in becoming the best leader possible, it is worth every second of your time and effort. We wish you the very best on your journey!

BIBLIOGRAPHY

Allen, J. (2004). *Difference Matters: Communicating Social Identity.* Long Grove, IL: Waveland Press.

Ambrus, A., Greiner, B., & Pathak, P. (2009). Group versus individual decision-making: Is th ere a shift? Institute for Advanced Study, School of Social Science Economics Working Paper, 91.

American Heart Association. (2003). National Center: Dallas, TX.

Belasco, J.A., & Stayer, R.C. (1993). *Flight of the Buffalo.* New York: Warner.

Benard, B. (2004). *Resiliency: What We Have Learned.* San Francisco, CA: West Ed.

Bennis, W., & Townsend, R. (1995). *Reinventing Leadership.* New York: Morrow Publishing.

Biography Channel Website. (2013). Clara Barton. Retrieved 01:45, October 16, 2013, from http://www.biography.com/people/clara-barton-9200960.

Block, P. (1987). *The Empowered Manager: Positive Skills at Work.* San Francisco: Jossey-Bass Limited.

Bokeno, R.M., & Gantt, V. (2000). Dialogic mentoring: Core relationships for organizational learning. *Management Communication Quarterly* 14(2): 237–270.

Bolman, L.G., & Deal, T.E. (1994). Looking for Leadership: Another Search Party's Report. *Educational Administration Quarterly*, *30*(1), 77–96.

Borisoff, D., & Victor, D. (1998). *Conflict Management: A Communication Skills Approach, 2nd ed.* Boston, MA: Allyn and Bacon.

Boverie, P. & Kroth. (2001). *Transforming Work: The Five Keys to Achieving Trust, Commitment, and Passion in the Workplace.* Cambridge, MA: Perseus Publishing.

Boverie, P., & Kroth. (2005). Motivation: Nine ways to create a more passionate work environment—starting today! Management File, Advancing Philanthropy (www.afnet.org).

Boylson, H.D. (1955). *Clara Barton: Founder of the American Red Cross.* New York: Random House.

Buber, M. (1970). *I and Thou.* New York: Charles Schribner's Sons.

Burns, J.M. (1978). *Leadership.* New York: Harper and Row.

Carnegie, D. (1885). *How to Enjoy Your Life and Your Job.* New York: Pocket Books.

Charactercounts.org. (2007).

Clinton, C. (2004). *Harriett Tubman: The Road to Freedom.* Boston: Little and Brown.

Covey, S. (1989). *The 7 Habits of Highly Effective People.* New York, NY: Simon & Schuster.

Covey, S. (1991). *Principle-Centered Leadership.* New York, NY: Summit Books.

Covey, S.R., Merrill, A.R., & Jones, D. (1998). *The Nature of Leadership.* Salt Lake City, Utah: Franklin Covey Company.

De Janasz, S., Dowd, K., & Schneider, B. (2002). *Interpersonal Skills in Organizations.* New York, NY: McGraw Hill Publications.

Depree, M. (1989). *Leadership is an Art.* New York: Doubleday.

De Vito, J. (2001). *The Interpersonal Communication Book,* 9th ed. New York: NY: Harper Collins Publishing.

DiSante, R. (2003). A prescription for faith: A conversation with Jeanne McCauley. *Research News & Opportunity in Science and Theology, 3*(3), 26–27.

Doswell, W.M., Kouyate, M., & Taylor, J. (2003). The role of spirituality preventing early sexual behavior. *American Journal of Health Studies, 70*(4), 195–202.

Dyer, W. (2012). *Wishes Fulfilled: Mastering the Art of Manifesting.* HayHouse USA, Carlsbad, CA.

Edginton, C.R., & Ford, P.F. (1985). *Leadership in Recreation and Leisure Service Organizations.* New York: John Wiley and Sons.

Edginton, C.R., Hudson, S.D., & Ford, P. (1999). *Leadership in Recreation and Leisure Service Organizations*, 2nd ed. Champaign, IL: Sagamore Publishing.

Eisenberg, E.M., & Goodall, Jr., H.L. (2004). *Organizational Communication,* 4th ed. Boston/New York: Bedford/St. Martin.

Eisler, R. (1995). *Sacred Pleasure.* New York: Harper Collins.

English, F.W. (1992). *Educational Administration: The Human Science.* New York: Harper Collins Publishing Company.

Frady, M. (2002). *Martin Luther King Jr: A Life.* New York, NY. Penguin Group.

French, J.P., Jr., & Raven, B. (1959). *The Basis of Social Power.* In D. Cartwright, ed. *Studies in Social Power.* Ann Arbor, MI: Institute for Social Research.

Fromm, E. (1956). *The Art of Loving: An Inquiry into the Nature of Love.* New York: Harper and Row.

Gächter, S., Nosenzo, D., Renner, E., & Sefton, M. (2012). Who Makes a Good Leader? Social Preferences and Leading-by-Example. *Economic Inquiry,* 50 (4), 867–879.

Gantt, V. (1997). Beneficial mentoring is for everyone: a reaction paper. Paper presented at the National Communication Association Convention, Chicago.

Gelb, M. (1998). *How to Think Like Leonardo da Vinci.* New York: Dell Publishing.

Gohm, C., & Clore, G. (2002). Affect as information: An individual-difference approach. In: Barrett, L., & Salovey, P., eds. The wisdom of feeling: Psychological processes in emotional intelligence. New York: Guilford Press; 89–113.

Gorrow, T., & Muller, S. (2008). The ABC's of Wellness for Teachers. Kappa Delta Pi, Indianapolis, IN.

Greenleaf, R.K. (1970). Indianapolis: The Robert Greenleaf Center.

Greenleaf, R.K. (1996). The Strategies of a Leader. In D.M. Frick and L.C. Spears, eds, *Focus on Leadership: Servant-leadership for the 21st Century,* 19–25. New York: John Wiley and Sons, Inc.

Hardy, J. (1984). *Managing for Impact in Nonprofit Organizations.* Erwin, TN: Essex Press.

Harrison, E.F. (1983). *Management and Organizations.* Boston: Houghton Mifflin Publishing.

Herman, M., Head, G., Jackson, P., & Fogarty, T. (2004). Managing risk in nonprofit organizations. Wiley, Hoboken, NJ.

Hersey, P., & Blanchard, K. (1977). *Management of Organizational Behavior— Utilizing Human Resources,* 3rd ed. Englewood Cliffs, NJ: Prentice-Hall.

Hesse, H. (1956). *Journey to the East.* New York: Noonday Press/Farrar Straus and Giroux.

Hitt, W.D. (1988). *The Leader Manager: Guidelines for Action.* Columbus, OH: Battelle Press.

Holander, E.P. (1978). What is the Crisis of Leadership? *Humanitas,* 14(3), 285–296.

Holt, C.L., Clark, E.M., Kreuter, M.W., & Rubio, D.M. (2003). Spiritual health locus of control and breast cancer beliefs among urban African American women. *Health Psychology, 22*(3), 294–302.

Homans, G.C. (1950). *The Human Group.* Harcourt, Brace and World.

House, R., Hanges, P. Javidan, J., Dorfman, P., & Gupta, V., eds. (2004). *Culture, Leadership, and Organizations: The GLOBE Study of 62 Societies.* Thousand Oaks, CA: Sage Publications.

(http://humanresources.about.com/od/involvementteams/a/team_culture.htm

Hunter, J.C. (1998). *The Servant: The Simple Story about the True Essence of Leadership.* New York: Crown Publishing Group.

Insel, P.M., & Roth, W.T. (2008). *Core Concepts in Health,* 10th ed. Boston: McGraw-Hill.

Ivancevich, J., & Matteson, M. (1980). *Stress and Work. A Managerial Perspective.* Glenview, IL: Scott Foresman.

Jackson, M., White, L., & Herman, M. (1997). *Mission Accomplished: The Workbook.* Washington, DC: Nonprofit Risk Management Center.

Jinkins, M. & Jinkins, D. (1998). *The Character of Leadership: Political Realism and Public Virtue in Nonprofit Organizations.* San Francisco: Jossey-Bass, Inc.

Katz, D., Maccoby, N., & Morse, N.C. (1950). *Productivity, Supervision and Morale in an Office Situation.* Ann Arbor: Survey Research Center, University of Michigan.

Katz, R.L. (1995). Skills of an Effective Administrator. *Harvard Business Review*, 33(1), 33–42.

Kelly, M. (2004). *The Rhythm of Life: Living Every Day with Passion & Purpose.* New York: Beacon Publishing.

Kelly, M. (2005). *The Seven Levels of Intimacy: The Art of Loving and the Joy of Being Loved.* New York, NY: Beacon Publishing.

KJV, *Provebs* 29:18. (1970). Camden, NJ: Thomas Nelson, Inc.

Koch, A., & Peden, P. (1993). *The Life and Selected Writings of Thomas Jefferson.* New York: Random House.

Konig, H.G. (2002). An 83-year-old woman with chronic illness and strong religious beliefs. *The Journal of the American Medical Association, 288,* 487–493.

Kotter, J.P. (May-June 1990). *What Leaders Really Do.* Harvard Business Review. Copyright by the President and Fellows of Harvard College, all rights reserved.

Kouzes, J.M. & Posner, B.Z. (2002). *The Leadership Challenge.* San Francisco, CA: John Wiley and Sons, Inc.

Kouzes, J.M., & Posner, B.Z. (2007). *The Leadership Challenge*, 4th ed. San Francisco: Jossey-Bass.

Kouzes, J.M., & Posner, B.Z. (2010). The Truth About Leadership: The No-Fads, Heart-of-the-Matter Facts You Need to Know. San Francisco: Jossey-Bass.

Kuh, G., & Whitt, E. (1988). The Invisible Tapestry: Culture in American Colleges and Universities. ASHE-ERIC Higher Education Reports 1988.

Levy, J.E. (1975). *Cesar Chavez: Autobiography of La Causa.* New York: W.W. Norton and Company, Inc.

Loeb, P.R. (2004). *The Impossible Will Take a Little Time.* New York: Perseus Books Group.

Luthans, F. (1967). *The Human Organization.* New York: McGraw-Hill.

MacIntyre, A.C. (1981). *After Virtue.* Notre Dame, IN: University of Notre Dame Press.

Maiers, A. (2009). Passion . . . a 21st Century Skill? You Decide! Retrieved from: http://www.angelamaiers.com/2009/05/passionization.html

Maslow, A.H. (1943). *Psychological Review,* July 370–96.

Maslow, A.H. (1954). *Motivation and Personality.* New York: Harper and Row.

Maxwell, J. (1993). *Developing the Leader Within You.* Nashville, TN: Thomas Nelson, Inc.

Maxwell, J. (1999). *The Indispensable Qualities of a Leader: Becoming the Person Others Will Want to Follow.* Nashville, TN: Thomas Nelson Publications.

Maxwell, J. (2004). *Today Matters: 12 Daily Practices to Guarantee Tomorrow's Success.* New York: Time Warner Book Group.

Meacham, J. (2012). *Thomas Jefferson: The Art of Power.* New York: Random House.

Miller, M. (2013). *The Heart of Leadership: Becoming a Leader People Want to Follow.* Barrett-Koehler Publishers, San Francisco, CA.

Montefiore, H. (2005). *Man and Nature: A Theological Assessment.* Zygon, 12: 199–211. doi: 10.1111/j.1467-9744.1977.tb00309.x

Nauert, R. (2013). Lab Research Finds Some Stress is Healthy. Psych Central. Retrieved from http://psychcentral.com/news/2013/04/18/lab-research-finds-some-stress-is-healthy/53855.html

Newman, J., & Grigg, D. (2007). Conducting a successful debriefing. Vancouver Sun, November 24. Retrieved from: http://www.working.com/vancouver/story. html?id=130519c7-f747-402d-bf1f-27b080afe8b6&k=10520

Northouse, P.G. (2007). *Leadership: Theory and Practice* (4th ed.). Thousand Oaks, CA: Sage Publications, Inc.

Ostrower, F., & Stone, M. (2006). Governance: research trends gaps and future prospects. In: Powell, W., Steinberg, R. (eds.) *The nonprofit sector: a research handbook.* 2nd ed. Yale University Press, New Haven, CT.

Owens, T., Stryker, S., & Goodman, N. (2001). *Extending Self-esteem theory and research.* Cambridge University Press, NY, NY.

Peck, M. S. (1978). *The Road Less Traveled: A New Psychology of Love, Traditional Values and Spiritual Growth.* New York: Simon & Schuster.

Peters, T.J., & Waterman, R.H. (1982). *In Search of Excellence.* New York: Harper and Row.

Petry, A. (1955). *Harriett Tubman.* New York: Thomas Y. Crowell Company.

Philbrick, N. (2010). *The Last Stand.* Viking Press: New York, NY.

Purkey, W.W. ,& Siegel, B. (2003). *Becoming an Invitational Leader: A New Approach to Professional and Personal Successes.* Atlanta: Humanics Trade Group Publication.

Raffoni, M. (2006). *Are You Spending Your Time the Right Way?* Boston, MA: Harvard Business School Publishing Co.

Reardon, K.K. (2007). Courage as a Skill. *Harvard Business Review,* January, 58–65.

Reddin, W.H. (1970). *Managerial Effectiveness.* New York: McGraw-Hill.

Relationship-Helps-And-Advice.com.

Richards, N. (1968). *People of Destiny, Helen Keller.* Chicago: Children's Press.

Riggio, R.E. (2009). Cutting-Edge Leadership: The best in current leadership research and theory, from cultivating charisma to transforming your organization. *Psychology Today.* Retrieved from: http://www.psychologytoday. com/blog/cutting-edge-leadership/200911/what-100-years-research-tells-us-about-effective-leadership

Rost, J.C. (1993). *Leadership for the Twenty-first Century.* Westport, CT: Praeger.

Ryckman, M. (2013). Advantages and Disadvantages of Stakeholders, *Houston Chronicle,* Hearst Communications, Ltd. Retrieved from: http://smallbusiness. chron.com/advantages-disadvantages-stakeholders-32179.html

Salovey, P., Rothman, A., Detweiler, J., & Steward, W. (2000). Emotional States and Physical Health. *American Psychologist*, 55(1).

Selye, H. (1976). Stress in health and disease. Reading, MA: Butterworth's.

Senge, P. (1990). *The Fifth Discipline: The Art and Practice of the Learning Organization.* New York, NY: Doubleday Publishing Co.

Seo, M. & Barrett, L. (2007). Being emotional during decision-making—Good or bad? An empirical investigation. *Acad Manage J.* August; 50(4): 923–940.

Sims, R.R., & Quatro, S.A., eds. (2005). *Leadership: Succeeding in the Private, Public, and Not-for-Profit Sectors.* Armonk, NY: M.E. Sharpe, Inc.

Stogdill, R. (1974). *Handbook of Leadership: A Survey of Theory and Research.* New York: Macmillan Company.

Stodgill, R., and Coons, A. (1975). *Leader Behavior's Description and Measurement.* Columbus: Bureau of Business Research, Ohio State University.

Tarafdar, M., Tu, Q., Ragu-Nathan, B., & Ragu-Nathan, T. (2007). The Impact of Technostress on Role Stress and Productivity. *Journal of Management Information Systems*, 24(1), 301–328. DOI: 10.2753/MIS0742-1222240109.

Thompson, A., & Cuseo, J. (2012). Infusing diversity and cultural competence into teacher education. Dubuque, IA: Kendall Hunt.

Tolle, E. (1997). *The Power of NOW: A Guide to Spiritual Enlightenment.* Novato, CA: New World Library.

Toffler, A. (1984). *Future Shock.* Bantam Books. New York, NY.

Tracy, B., & Chee, P. (2013). *12 Disciplines of Leadership Excellence: How Leaders Achieve Sustainable High Performance.* McGraw-Hill, New York, NY.

Utley, R.M. (1988). *Cavalier in Buckskin.* Norman: University of Oklahoma Press.

Van der Smissen, B. (1990). *Legal Liability and Risk Management for Public and Private Entities* (Vol. 2). Cincinnati, OH.

Vroom, V.H. & Yetton, P.W. (1973). *Leadership and Decision Making.* Pittsburg, PA: University of Pittsburg Press.

Weis, R. (1998). *Service Learning Training Manual for Faculty K–16.* Murray, KY: American Humanics, Murray State University.

Weis, R., and Gantt, V. (2002). *Leadership and Program Development in Nonprofit Organizations.* Peosta, IA: Eddie Bowers Publishing Company.

Weis, R., & Gantt, V. (2004). *Knowledge and Skill Development in Nonprofit Organizations.* Peosta, IA: Eddie Bowers Publishing Company.

Weis, R. & Gantt, V. (2009). *Leading with Character, Purpose and Passion*. Kendall Hunt: Dubuque, Iowa.

Weis, R., Rogers, K., and Broughton, J. (2004). Selecting and training staff and volunteer members for leadership, character, and competencies. *Journal of Volunteer Administration,* 22 (1), 38–4.

Wellness in Your Life. (2005). South Deerfield, MA: Channing Bete Company.

Wolf, T. (1999). *Managing a Nonprofit Organization in the Twenty-First Century. Simon & Schuster* New York, NY.

Wren, J. Thomas. (1995). *The Leaders's Companion.* New York: The Free Press.

www.eatright.org.; www.nal.usda.gov/fnic.

Your Guide to Human Resources.

Zoglio. S. (1993). *Seven Keys to Building Great Workteams.* Available online. <http// www.teambuildinginc.com> (select: "Articles"; select: "7 Keys to Building Great Work teams").

AUTHORS' PAGE

Roger M. Weis, Ed.D. is Professor for the Nonprofit Leadership Studies program at Murray State University (MSU). He has twice been selected as student advisor of the year and was the first recipient of the American Humanics National Award for Excellence in Leadership and the first recipient of the Distinguished Service Learning and Civic Engagement Award at MSU. During his tenure, the NLS program at MSU has received numerous national and local awards for excellence in academics, leadership, service, and research and has been the largest program in the country for quite some time.

Dr. Weis has also served as chair of the American Humanics Directors Association for two terms and on the AH National Board of Directors for two terms. He is the founding chair of the Big Brothers Big Sisters program in Murray, the Campus Connection Volunteer Center, and the MSU Center for Service Learning and Civic Engagement and the founding co-chair of the Service Learning Scholars program and the Health Matters for Students program. Previously, he has had eight books published, six of which are textbooks dealing in part with leadership. He has presented leadership workshops and forums to youth, human service, and other organizations and has lectured and made presentations to over 100 institutions of education around the world including Oxford and Cambridge Universities in England and Trinity College in Ireland.

Susan Marie Muller, Professor of Health Education at Murray State University, is a Master Certified Health Education Specialist (MCHES). She earned her doctorate in Health Education from the University of Maryland College Park and has thirty-one years of teaching experience including nine years as a middle and elementary school health instructor, and twenty-two years as a college professor. She has held several leadership positions over the past two decades, most notably, as the Dean, College of Health Sciences and Human Services (HSHS) at Murray State University and as an academic department chairperson at Salisbury University. In these positions, she has demonstrated the leadership concepts promoted in this book: ethical leadership and skill in human and financial resource management; fostering others in teaching, research, and professional development; and promoting the values of shared governance as the means to advance the academy.

CPSIA information can be obtained
at www.ICGtesting.com
Printed in the USA
LVHW061130151118
597190LV00004B/11/P